T0368087

SOuL
ENERGY
FROM
THE
HEART

The WAY and the WORK
to Heal Your Trauma and
Love Your Life

Volume 1

JASON BOAL

BALBOA.PRESS
A DIVISION OF HAY HOUSE

Balboa Press books may be ordered through booksellers or by contacting:

Balboa Press
A Division of Hay House
1663 Liberty Drive
Bloomington, IN 47403
www.balboapress.com
844-682-1282

Because of the dynamic nature of the Internet, any web addresses or links contained in this book may have changed since publication and may no longer be valid. The views expressed in this work are solely those of the author and do not necessarily reflect the views of the publisher, and the publisher hereby disclaims any responsibility for them.

The author of this book does not dispense medical advice or prescribe the use of any technique as a form of treatment for physical, emotional, or medical problems without the advice of a physician, either directly or indirectly. The intent of the author is only to offer information of a general nature to help you in your quest for emotional and spiritual well-being. In the event you use any of the information in this book for yourself, which is your constitutional right, the author and the publisher assume no responsibility for your actions.

Any people depicted in stock imagery provided by Getty Images are models, and such images are being used for illustrative purposes only. Certain stock imagery © Getty Images.

Print information available on the last page.

ISBN: 979-8-7652-5855-2 (sc)
ISBN: 979-8-7652-5854-5 (e)

Library of Congress Control Number: 2024926367

Balboa Press rev. date: 12/13/2024

Contents

Foreword

The Four Horsemen. That's what we call ourselves. Not of some apocalypse, but of a bond of friendship that has lasted for just short of fifty years. Jason and I are two of those Four Horsemen. When you know someone for as long as we have, you tend to learn a thing or two about each other.

What have I learned about your author? For one, he's smart. Smarter than me. The kind of smart that continuously lands you on the dean's list. But also the kind of smart that has awakened in this world. Jason knows his place in the universe. He's worked hard to understand not only who he is, but what he is and why. Most people in life don't even bother to ask the big questions. The questions that really matter. The thoughts that propel us forward in life, ready to surmount the next challenge, always with an opportunity for growth.

Jason and I really amped up our friendship around twenty-five years ago when we both dived deep into our respective journeys. We've had an endless number of phone calls and texts over those years. Conversations about the universe and our place in it. Meditation, tai chi, Zen, the Law of One, and spirituality in general. Our journeys differed in ways, but we always knew that whatever those differences were, we were all essentially on the same path. It was just a question of how you chose to get there.

You'll learn in the pages to follow that Jason is not without challenge. He's overcome adversity in his journey. Alcoholism, anger, divorce—all have played out in his life. The beauty is that he was smart enough to see his issues as catalysts. An opportunity for change. And he lays these events out for you in such a manner that you too may also have that opportunity to make a different choice.

Jason will walk you through his journey in this book. He'll show you how he grew. Turning tumultuous situations into growth opportunities one after the other. He'll introduce you to Sol. Whether he's a guide, a friend, or a piece of Jason's consciousness— it doesn't really matter. The two of them take you on a journey like no other, intertwining the waking world with the depths of the mind.

I deeply respect my friend. His ability to overcome hardships, walk through those experiences with full awareness and learn from them, is truly a gift. His life could have taken a very different path. But it didn't. It didn't because of his determination to find a better way. In my life I allow the universe to determine the next part of my journey. The next book I read is almost always a result of the book I'm reading. Allowing yourself to flow with the energy, not against it. If you're here reading this, it's not out of coincidence or serendipity. It's because at this time in *your* adventure; this is what *you* need.

Enjoy the journey.
Kerr Smith

Preface

This book is all about finding the joy and happiness that resides inside each one of us and not looking externally for that joy and happiness. It truly is the only way, and it is the common thread among all spiritual disciplines and religions. I am sharing my experiences, wisdom, and tools that I have discovered to help me stay on this path in my life.

This book is also about me being vulnerable. Some of the content and my story is very personal information that I have not shared with many other people, including my journey with addiction, my divorce, and my arrest. This book also includes intricate details from my dreams that I have documented over the past twenty-plus years. I have always been fascinated by dreams, and my dreams are typically very detailed, vivid, and well, just plain crazy sometimes. I am so intrigued about the fact that we can have completely separate life experiences and journeys after we close our eyes for sleep. In my opinion, our dreams are connected to a common universal thread of energy and will tell us very insightful and helpful things about our lives.

My hope is that my sharing will help you in whatever journey you are currently experiencing. I know for me, personally, being vulnerable has truly humbled me and helped me in my own journey.

The book does not follow the normal format of a book, and that is by design. I will take you through a journey between the way and the work and my subconscious mind. Here is some additional context to help you in understanding the format and flow of the book.

The Way. These sections are meant for contemplating and are more philosophical in nature.

The Work. These sections are meant for doing and are more action related. These are the tools that I use daily, such as meditating twice daily and taking cold showers.

Sol. Follow Sol through the unconscious depths of my mind, as he has come to me with purpose. I have documented my dreams over the past twenty-plus years. Sol is the conduit between my dream and conscious states, and he appeared to me during a manifesting meditation telling me both his name and his symbol (a solar day on Mars). His journey is indicated by the parts in this book that have a month and year preceding the content. The dates are approximations, as Sol does not have a timeline of his own life. In most cases, the way and the work content that directly follows each of Sol's dream sequences is tied in to how I derived meaning from my dreams.

Introduction

Trust in dreams, for in them is hidden the gate to eternity.
—Kahlil Gibran

Here I am. I find myself.

Sitting on my front porch watching the rain come down, I am gratefully protected from the wind and wetness. It's perfection outside.

The trees are getting exactly what they need right now. The grass is getting exactly what it needs right now.

And so, in turn, I am getting exactly what I need right now.

The moment is beautiful; it's perfect and doesn't require anything. So, I sit here feeling the energy in my body from the storm and from nature's amazing creations. The smell of the rain keeps me connected to the beauty of it all.

Life is good.

Let's begin our journey together—a journey toward understanding and healing and returning home to yourself.

As you read through this, I would like to request that you keep two visualizations or ideas in mind. I am a believer in the ability of visualizations to improve your life, as you will soon discover.

First, our natural state is emptiness and love. Our minds are spacious and vast. They are empty first and foremost. From that emptiness grows infinite potential. Our minds are very powerful. Use this force wisely.

Second, I want you to picture yourself floating down a river in the most carefree state that you can imagine. We are meant to float with the currents of life. Have there been times in your own life when you have subtly gone against the current, or even gotten out of the water, and felt like you were fighting against your current life experience? These are the moments to return to the carefree state of floating in your river, whatever that may look like.

Sidestepping one of the most dangerous situations of my life, I almost lost my freedom. Well, I did lose my freedom for a short time. I wouldn't label it a near-death experience, but part of me died that day. A part of me that needed to die, so that I could truly be free.

It was a sliding-glass-door moment in my life.

There are moments in life that need to be examined, cared for, and analyzed. They need to be accepted and then fully let go. This was that moment for me.

It was the way. I had to do the work. As a human being existing on this planet, life was preparing me to handle that exact moment. It has been a constant drive of mine to become a more loving, open-hearted, and connected person. Desperately longing to align my intentions to the highest energy levels, I discovered that I need to be of greater service to the world at large.

During that moment sitting on the bare jail cell floor, I brought the way and the work together in perfect unison. I practiced my tai chi to circulate my chi energy and keep alive. I practiced my Transcendental Meditation (TM) to ground myself and not ruminate on the potential charges looming. I learned TM directly after my divorce as a tool to help me get through it. During that time, I practiced TM two times a day for twenty minutes for three straight years. I didn't miss a day or session, no matter where I was. I practiced on planes, in lobbies, in taxis, anywhere I needed to.

While in jail, I also practiced my ChiRunning to keep my body moving and my mind still. I opened my heart and connected to the homeless young man in need when I gave my yin and yang necklace to him to help him through his suicidal situation.

November 1998

Sol excitedly walked down toward Pat's Cheesesteaks, where he knew from experience the cooks were the best. The old woman shot him a quick smile and wink and served him up the best Philly cheesesteak he had eaten in years. He took his food down to the tables, where others were gathered. Sol received a text from one of his bosses which read, "You're doing OK." Interestingly enough, this happened at the same exact moment another boss was talking to everyone at his table.

As Sol left Pat's, he helped the cook take the garbage out back, as he'd been doing for four years since the divorce. She helped anyway; she always did. She didn't, however, understand why he hesitated when she offered her help. He didn't either, really. He had nothing to hide, not at this point in his life. He'd come so far with everything, though some scar tissue remained.

Sol realized that fear was causing him to avoid certain aspects of his life and thus he was not living life fully to his own satisfaction.

THE WAY

Beyond Fear and the Ego

I discovered what was on the other side of fear, of death, and of my ego. It was a scary place to be for a while. Something about it felt so incredibly real and right. My true calling in life was being awakened. It was if I was returning to my soul, shedding all the pain, tearing down my walls, and letting go of my past traumas.

I always knew there was a way. There had to be a way. This is the only logical conclusion that made sense to me. At the same time, I also know what I have experienced directly. This lifetime of experiences has validated that there is a way for me, and that there is also a way for you. I have often thought that I was missing something, and this feeling plagued me for years. Has the way simply been in me, around me, everywhere, all along? Ruminating over so many questions for years that I didn't have answers to was frustrating yet fueled my search with fiery intensity.

So, I sit. I sit with myself, in silence. I create a space for the answers, for the way, to appear. Quieting everything gives the way a space to show itself. Synchronicities occur, and I experience moments of enlightenment when I truly pay attention to my intuition. My true soul is now revealed.

I am patient; I have to be. I have no other choice.

I know enough to realize this is true.

June 1988

It rained so hard that day that the fish swam out of the pond into his yard. Sol quickly grabbed two bass and tossed them back in, knowing they may come back out again. The dock was covered in water, not to be seen. It only rained for a few hours, but seven inches came down. The rain eventually let up and moved up the coastline to another town.

The birds came back out, and the sound of traffic started moving through the valley again. The sun dumped out its ray of light through a hole the clouds created for it. The hole seemed to suck up energy from the trees and life below.

Sol was beginning to understand that no matter how many fish he tried to save that day, he couldn't save them all. He had to save himself first for him to help others in need.

THE WAY

My Rock Bottom

I stumbled in a big, big way. I couldn't drive my son to his flag football event that night, the day before his eighth birthday. I had too much to drink. I was in a dark spot in my life. My priorities were out of order. Heck, my mind was out of order. I had no center, no balance, no strength, no fortitude. I wasn't living life; I was skidding through it, with danger around each day.

That night changed my life; it was the true beginning of digging myself out, of setting myself straight. Realizing that I was jeopardizing the safety of my son through my reckless and careless attitude about myself, and my situation was my rock bottom. It made me sick to my stomach, the thought that I would do this to my son, an innocent child I would take a bullet for and move the earth for any time, any place. It was as if I was doing this to my younger self. This cognitive dissonance was too loud this time, thank God. So, I continued along my long journey of finding myself and reconnecting with who I used to be when I was younger, before the childhood trauma.

When I was younger, I was carefree, spontaneous, curious, and lived each day with an open heart connected to everyone and everything. I had energy in spades and looked forward to the adventures that every day seemed to magically bring to me.

Coming up on twelve years of sobriety next month, I have

now returned to myself. I can honestly say that I love myself and every moment of life to the best of my ability. I am grateful for the myriad chances that I have been given to reach this spot in my life experience. I thank God and the universe every single day for my sobriety and the second chance that has been given to me.

May 1991

Sol stepped into the crowed auditorium. It was packed, with almost every seat taken already, and there were still thirty minutes until the ceremony would start. He wasn't prepared for this, so he had to think quickly. He knew the cadets were looking to him for guidance and possibly motivation. He delivered his ideas, and the cadets were engaged and willing to move forward. His team members, however, were a different story. They weren't expecting him to take over so soon. They were surprised and caught off guard by the new direction that he was heading. This would take some time to repair.

Fortunately, Marc D. was there to help. They had played travel club soccer together in middle and high school. Marc was by far his favorite teammate and friend on the team. Aside from being a great teammate, he was an even better leader. They were going to make a great team here, and Mark appeared to be fully on board with supporting the new direction.

Sol thought afterward that if he hadn't got out of his own way and let Mark help with the situation, then things would not have turned out as well as they did.

Get Out of the Way

While on a work trip in San Antonio, Texas, I was standing with a very good friend and mentor at the time, overlooking the River Walk and enjoying a pleasant early evening conversation before the group dinner. At this point in my life, my early thirties, I felt stuck both personally and professionally. My friend could sense my frustration and confusion and overall depressed attitude. He listened carefully as I talked and didn't really say much. Then, right before we headed out, he said, "Jason, you just need to get the fuck out of your own way." He really did have a way of saying things. At first, I got defensive. Later that night after dinner, as I was winding down and reflecting on my day as I often do, I realized he was coming from a place of love and caring and that he was spot on! He wanted me to be the best version of myself, not only for the agency he owned but also for me. I will be forever grateful for that moment.

I often thought that I was the problem. Maybe I was in the way somehow. Not just in the way of others and their happiness but also in my own way. I have learned from my twenty-five years of meditating that I was blocking the answer that I was seeking. I was not doing this on purpose, of course; I simply thought that I was the one who had to work hard to find the answer. I thought I had to find the answer through force, by doing a certain something or thinking a certain way.

Take some time to determine whether there is any place in your life where you feel stuck right now. It could be something small, such as not doing the laundry, or something bigger, such as eating a healthier diet. Now what if you could actually get out of your own way? How? Realize that your thoughts and beliefs could very well be dragging you down and impeding your progress. Write down the common thoughts that keep popping into your head about these issues. For each thought, tie it to a belief that you may have about that specific topic. For example, I may be thinking, *I can't believe I actually have to do two more loads of laundry today. Is this what my life is coming down to, laundry?* Now as a single dad, I have done hundreds and hundreds of loads of laundry, so this was definitely a common thought at times.

What if I changed my belief about doing laundry to something healthier, such as, *I am enabling my three children to wear clean clothes and feel good about themselves throughout their day.* Wow, what a shift! This is how I view doing laundry now. I am grateful for the opportunity to care for my children this way. I didn't always feel that way, and it took time and reflection to get to where I am now. Simply by reflecting on my thoughts and my beliefs linked to those thoughts allowed me to get out of my own way. It can be this easy.

April 1994

Sol was putting his lacrosse gloves and arm pads on before practice. It was great to talk with his coach and see his teammates during line drills. He couldn't, however, figure out how the hell he was going to run in the snow during the game. He tested out different parts of the field; in one place, the snow was up to his knees. He'd figure out a way; he always did.

The storm was here, the winds blowing so hard the front

door to the house had to be pulled with all his weight to shut it completely. A pillow blew off the porch and into the yard, and Sol ran after it before leaving. Right after grabbing the pillow, Sol had the sudden urge to stand motionless in the rain, winds, and storm. It was almost as if an invisible force or energy was keeping him in place just a few moments longer. A sense of awe and wonder overcame Sol as he marveled at his direct experience of the magic of the universe and took everything in with all his senses.

THE WAY

Forest Bathing

There is a Japanese concept called forest bathing where you spend time in nature and simply sit. My girlfriend, Maureen, and I do this several times a week. It has an incredibly positive impact on how the rest of our day turns out. During this process of sitting and just being, we take a few minutes to close our eyes and to just be in the moment and allow the vastness and stillness of the forest to take front stage. Then, when it feels right, we open our eyes and pay attention to the sounds, the smells, the sights. It could be looking at an amazing spider web that seems to suspend itself in the middle of the air or smelling freshly fallen trees. There is something healthy, healing, and magical about breathing in the oxygen-rich air from the trees and quieting our minds for a bit.

When I cannot make it out to a forest or park, I will often sit on my front porch to meditate, manifest, and simply connect with something greater than myself. Oftentimes birds will fly over and land very close to me. One day, a smaller bird flew over and sat on the branch and began to clean its feathers. I contemplated and experienced the moment, which I do a lot out here. The bird was not thinking about his bad childhood. Not even aware of a childhood. The bird doesn't worry about stupid shit. The bird simply is. It hops, looks for food, eats, and then flies away. It's that simple.

I understand now that there is something about me, in me, of me, that has enabled me to weather all my storms. Storms such as being laid off from two different jobs that I loved: one during the very early stages of my separation and the other very recently. Heavy thoughts would creep in, including how in the world I would support myself and my three children financially. Storms such as surviving childhood trauma. Storms such as hurting other people during my addictions. This something inside of me is greater than my scars and hurts and abandonments. Experiencing my true inner strength, my resolve, and ability to weather these dark storms has led me to one of my truths, something I know to be true through experience. It's magical. Life is meant to be understood and experienced, and we are here for only a moment to share our gifts and love with others. Finding my truth has truly enabled me to realize this and live this daily. I truly wish the same for you.

I have learned also not to worry about the stupid shit. It only brings me down and keeps me from fully experiencing and enjoying my life. There's no point in worrying about certain things. I start to understand the way more and more each day. The good feelings—like sitting on the porch reading and enjoying the quiet summer day watching the clouds and cars and birds go by—don't last. And the bad feelings—stressful workdays with phone calls and client stress—don't last either.

In fact, I take it a step further and understand that neither of the two above examples are good or bad; they just are. This lightens me up a lot. It simplifies things for me. Just be—without the labels. Just experience—without the labels and judgments. Why is this so hard for us humans sometimes? Take some time every day, if possible, to get outside and connect with nature. Listen to the birds, watch the wind blow through the trees, contemplate the clouds. This will help you quiet your mind over time and connect you to something much bigger than yourself.

December 2009

Sol always found it to share a joint with a friend. How you hold it, how you breathe and talk, the things you talk about, how you pass it. He realized that they had to get quickly get out of that room. It felt like it was 110 degrees in there, and they'd been in there for the better part of three hours. How could no one else want to get up and leave? Maybe they did. So, he snuck out to the garage in the house, not knowing his friend did the same.

They shared laughs and a few stories, until the party next store noticed them. Well, that guy either wanted to call the cops or join us. Later that day, he needed guidance to tiptoe through the dark room to avoid all the obstacles on the floor. He was leaving the firm he'd been with for the past ten years. His good buddy was the head of the firm and took it hard, badly, really. Sol hugged the secretary to say goodbye. When he went to shake his boss's hand, his boss said to leave, the sooner the better. It stung, but he knew it was coming from a place of lost love, a place of hurt. He understood. They'd talk again later in life. Sol realized that many times in life the obstacles in front of him are not real and that if he simply continues walking forward each day then things will be OK.

THE WAY

Gateless Gate

My favorite collection of Zen koans is the *Gateless Gate*. If you're not familiar with koans, they are meant to be contemplated and experienced. There is no intellectual answer. *The Gateless Gate* is a collection of forty-eight (Zen) koans compiled in the early thirteenth century by the Chinese Zen master Wumen Huikai during the Song dynasty.

Meditating on and contemplating the idea of a gateless gate for many years (my email address even starts with *gateless gate*!), I began to understand that I was indeed the barrier. I was in the way of my own enlightenment. I was a gate when I didn't have to be a gate. Now I manifest and experience expansiveness and openness. We are literally the universe. Close your eyes and stare into the darkness. Quiet your mind. Do this daily and you may start to experience the same that I do daily. There is infinite potential and possibilities in our minds, if you're not a gate.

Gateless gate—there is no gate though I thought there was a gate. When I experienced that there is no gate, I understood. I discovered that I didn't have to do or force anything—that was the way. I just needed to be, to experience life as it is, in its raw, beautiful, unadulterated format. So now I am not in a hurry so much anymore. My mom would always say, "Slow down, Jason," but I never knew what she meant because she never explained it on a level that I would understand. Now, I slow down more, because I know there's nowhere to go, nothing to chase, to get or obtain. I already have it—no—I already am it. It is the universe, the cosmos, and I am part of it, and it is part of me. It's all one. No separation. No struggling. No confusion.

May 2009

Sol had to speak up. He had something important to share, something he had directly experienced years ago. He spoke with confidence and projected his voice, but didn't raise it. Others were making eye contact, and he realized he was connecting and making a difference. After he finished, he realized he had interrupted a previous presentation that had begun. But people listened when he gave his talk. They needed to hear it. When the evening's events wrapped up, he had to be careful. He was not at all interested in sleeping in the woods with no cover, no bedding, no safety. The snakes in the area were made of legend. So, he traveled around the campsite from group to group, talking and listening. Watching the fires die away to red embers, and then to just a fizzle of smoke. He had to figure out what he would do for the next five hours. Mostly, where he would sleep. Sol realized at this moment that he needed more guidance and wisdom to help him through this situation and wondered how he could obtain that information.

THE WORK

Find Your Spirit Animal

My spirit animal is the white wolf, which I discovered through Dakota Earth Cloud Walker "Rise of the Phoenix" guided mediation on Insight Timer. I am forever grateful to Dakota for sharing her creativity and soul on Insight Timer. If you have ever thought about spirit animals and are curious as to what yours could be, then absolutely give this guided meditation some space in your practice. Dakota doesn't guarantee that you'll find your spirit animal, but I would not at all be surprised if you did. Give it some time and keep an open mind. It took me several sessions to find my white wolf.

My white wolf has been a source of inspiration and courage to me for many years now. I often see her in my meditations, and I have called upon her strength and guidance in many situations in my life. White wolves are not afraid of humans but do approach them cautiously. They are fierce hunters and fast runners, often hunting alone in the summer yet living in packs and caring for their pups. It is almost a bit eerie how many traits I share with the white wolf.

Depending upon my situation, I will conjure my spirt animal and ask her for guidance and support and strength. I will sit with her during meditation, just sit in silence with her. Sometimes she will start to move and dance and hunt, and other times she will circle around me providing protection and safety. There are times, however, when she appears without any effort whatsoever on my part. These are my favorite times with her. She appears mostly through her head and face at first, as a powerful strong and large visualization. She is right in front of me, staring deeply into my heart and soul with her beautiful, magical eyes. Each time this happens, I listen intently with all my being, and then when it is over, I give thanks to her for showing herself and sharing her gifts with me.

November 1998

They left the restaurant and hopped into Sol's car. The parking spaces were way too tight to get out comfortably. Sol slightly tapped the white car next to him on his way out, which one of the workers saw. They directed him over to the exit booths where they forced each car through a car wash option. It was actually a great scam, as most customers, like himself, just went along with their direction and drove over to the station. Sol was sure there was another way out. Once he got there, they began to tell him that he owed them money for the damaged car, and that his state inspection sticker was on the wrong window, and that he'd have to pay hundreds of dollars to have that changed. He asked for the manager, who quickly came over and resolved this situation.

Somehow Sol got the car going backward on the freeway. He slowed down and the car behind him skidded into them, banging the front grille of the car pretty good. Another SUV flew by and swiped the side of the car, making a loud screeching sound. No one could stop. The traffic was just too fast on the freeway at this time of the day. He just had to make it past the semitrailer truck next to him. A few more seconds. When he got past the truck, he spun the car around to the right direction and sped off. That was close. The guy in the pickup truck was not happy at all about the whole scenario, as he almost got caught up in the mess. The guy flicked him the bird as he sped away.

Sol ended up pulling into a minimart as he was deciding how he would meet up with his college buddy Press. He was in town for a few days, and they hadn't seen each other in years. The cashier asked if he could pay fifteen dollars with ones. He thought, *Huh?* but he had the change, so he helped her out a bit. Sol sat for a few moments soaking up the sunlight on a bench outside the minimart. He sat and let his thoughts come without judgment or response or action. He was curious whether he could find the answer for his plans simply by sitting and listening. As he left the store and turned the corner, he ran smack into Jason. What were the odds, in such a big city, to meet like this? They caught up and planned the next few days. He was excited for their plans.

Holding Space for Yourself

You may have heard of the concept of holding space for someone else as they go through and experience difficult feelings. If you haven't heard of it before, it's actually quite simple. You simply be a presence for that other person. Just be there for them. Just listen. Create more space for them; don't hog space. When you hold space, you don't judge or interrupt or provide solutions. Although it sounds rather simple, it is very challenging in practice. At some point today, try it with someone you love. It really is an act of love to do this with another person.

What if you flipped that script and held space for yourself? What an amazing act of self-love that would be! You can do this as uncomfortable feelings arise. Notice how your body feels when these negative feelings pay you a visit. Where does it show in your body physically? Now do a quick experiment with yourself. I absolutely love experiments! Hold space for yourself for three minutes. Follow the guidelines above about holding space for someone else. After three minutes is up, reassess yourself. What does it feel like to you internally and in your body now, after you've held space for yourself? Do you feel any lighter?

What if the angst that you feel on a day-to-day basis, the constant hum of anxiety, the reason you dream so much about anxiety and stress, is because something inside of you needs to come out?

Continue to hold space each day for yourself in whatever form works best for you. It could be meditation, running, walking, music—whatever it is, start to practice this daily. Build this habit out. It will transform your life and your relationships, starting with the most important relationship, the one with yourself.

June 2024

Sol walked down to the ocean by finding the small boardwalk that led through the dunes. The sky looked angry and peaceful at the same time. It was beautiful, a deep dark blue and purple color, and the waves were active. He wondered how many times he'd been down here before. This time seemed much different though. Something felt different inside of him. Afterward, he went back to the shop, where they were closing up. Everything had to be inventoried and accounted for by the end of that night. He hadn't experienced any robberies or thefts at his store; it's just how he preferred to run his business. His recent best-selling book on friendships had been the hot item lately. Sol started to feel like he belonged. Like he truly, truly belonged here. Part of the cosmos, part of the family, part of existence. He felt connected now, like nothing was missing. It was a novel feeling for him, to experience the truth of not needing anything outside of himself to feel whole, to feel OK, to feel content. It was as if an invisible and powerful energy was flowing from the universe into him and through his body and then back out to the universe again. It seemed like a beautiful and mysterious dance to him.

THE WAY

Emptiness

We are so very busy these days. Especially in the Western world. I started my meditation practice over twenty-five years ago. The allure of the quietness of the East, the mysticism and interesting energy component to understanding myself was what attracted me most. Tai chi was a part of that for me as well.

I taught myself tai chi during COVID-19 and practiced religiously every day for two years. Early in the morning I would get into beginner's stance, with Finn, my rottweiler puppy, at my feet. He would stay there and chew his bone for thirty to forty-five minutes while I practiced. To this day, I believe my tai chi practice had a major impact on Finn's personality. Anyone who has had the pleasure of meeting Finn understands what I mean. Finn's AKC name is Gentle Tai Chi Giant, and it fits him perfectly.

I learned the art of circulating and activating my internal chi energy. Tai chi is a moving meditation practice and fit me perfectly because of my drive to quiet my mind while also keeping my body moving and active. Something amazing happens inside when you work with your chi. Chi, according to traditional Chinese medicine, is the fuel and essence that connects body, mind, and spirt. Master Waysun Liao, in his book *Restoring Your Life Energy* says that without chi we fall apart physically, mentally, and spiritually. I believe to this be very true through my own personal experiences and tai chi practice. When I move my chi with deliberate intent, an aliveness comes over me. During my practice, I could feel my energy moving inside of my body. At times—and this sounds absolutely crazy, but it happened—my hands and arms would stay afloat during a stance without any effort on my part whatsoever. It was during these times when I truly believed in chi energy and how vital it is to us as humans.

Another amazing effect that would happen during my practice was that I could feel energy between my hands when they were three to four feet apart in front of me. The movement involves imagining a ball of energy between your hands and that is what you hold throughout some of the movements. The energy ball would shrink or grow, many times without a conscious use of force on my part. Again, I experienced firsthand how real our chi energy within our bodies is.

To this day, when I am feeling sick, which I rarely am, I circulate my chi from my dantian to the part of my body that needs healing. The dantian is located just below your navel about an inch inside your body. It is not an organ or a physical thing. It is the source of your chi, where all life energy is summoned and circulated. I use a technique called condensing breathing that I learned during my training. The breathing is done with purpose and intent, and again visualizations are employed during the inhale to "condense" your skeletal bones to the marrow. When I practice this method, I can feel the energy growing stronger in my body. I believe 100 percent that I have the ability to heal myself with my own internal energy.

The other amazing benefit to my tai chi practice is that my mind and body become one. I am no longer stuck in my head. I become somewhat empty inside. When we are truly empty, we have no negative stories in our head. And we have no positive stories either. It is just pure emptiness, exactly like when we were born. This is our natural state. If you do the work, which I have done and continue to do daily, I believe you can easily tap into this blank space and create whatever you want in life. And you guessed it, I am going to remind you that it takes daily practice, new habits, and a strong desire to want this deep understanding of yourself and your purpose here on earth.

September 2021

It wasn't nighttime yet, but the roads were getting darker by the minute. Sol was driving down the street only going about twenty-five miles per hour when he noticed a man up ahead in the road. He slowed to fifteen miles per hour as he approached the man. In his arms, the man appeared to be carrying a large, wounded animal; it almost looked like a hyena. Sol got closer and came to a stop to let the man cross the street. The man was standing in the middle of the street but didn't make eye contact. In his arms was an older child, maybe in his teens. The man was carrying him in a way that looked like he had been carrying him all day. He passed the man slowly, looked in his rear review mirror, and noticed that the man had now put the boy down, and the boy was walking, or at least trying to walk. The boy was handicapped, or something had happened to him earlier in his life.

Sol then walked across the city street toward the store where he purchased the concert tickets. A man in his late forties stopped him in the street. He asked, "Hey, were you planning on going to that concert Thursday night?" Why yes, he was. He had just purchased the tickets two days prior and was walking over to pick them up. The man said, "He left for Brooklyn this morning. No concert. Take it easy, man." *Brooklyn?* he thought. He didn't know he was from Brooklyn. He was disappointed to say the least.

He walked back across the street to the deli. The Indian lady next to him had an order and a half of dinner all lined up in bags ready to go, and it looked delicious. He ordered the usual and looked for something extra for dessert. He smiled at the Indian lady, and then went home for the night.

As he walked home, a wave of intense gratitude come over him for the events that just transpired. From the chance encounter with the man about the concert tickets to the pleasant exchange of smiles with the older lady. He forgot about all his worries during this moment of true appreciation.

THE WORK

Gratitude

This being human is a guest house. Every morning is a new arrival. A joy, a depression, a meanness, some momentary awareness comes as an unexpected visitor.... Welcome and entertain them all. Treat each guest honorably. The dark thought, the shame, the malice, meet them at the door laughing, and invite them in. Be grateful for whoever comes, because each has been sent as a guide from beyond.
—Rumi

I am not a huge fan of words mostly because I feel that they restrict our experiences. I realize that sounds crazy coming from a writer and a lover of books and learning. However, the word *gratitude* is one of the most powerful and important words in my daily life and meditation practice.

We have so much to be grateful for. Every single day. We have so much. We forget about all that we have when we get caught up in our negative thought patterns, our stories from the past that are seriously embedded within us, and our emotions which seem uncontrollable at times. When you wake up tomorrow morning, before getting out of bed and doing anything, take stock of what words and thoughts and feelings automatically flood your being. Where is gratitude on that list? Does it appear? If not, take a few moments before getting out of bed to feel grateful for a few things in your life right now. Notice I said feel and not think grateful. Joe Dispenza is amazing at teaching the concept of tying new feelings to your inner experience. You must feel what gratitude feels like. Feel what it's like to be grateful for the bed and blanket you just slept in. Maybe the roof over your head or the food in your fridge. It only takes a few minutes each day to do this, and the results will absolutely astound you over time.

If I can catch myself in a funk, and then bring gratitude immediately into my life, things change around me almost instantly. I immediately feel better inside. I invite you to get super curious and experiment with your life if you are looking for more. If you can build the habit doing the work, each day, over and over, I feel that you will discover magic along your journey. Magic about yourself and magic about experiencing life in general. Try not to get frustrated or bored by the work. Disciplined work will always pay off in the long run. It's going to open your life up to incredible new levels of living and experiencing yourself and others. I am so excited for you right now.

One of the first things I do at the start of every meditation, before a hot yoga class, and before a run is to express my thanks to God for the abundance that I am surrounded by each and every day. This includes the warmth of my bed at night, the food in my pantry, the love from others, the health of my children. This list goes on and on. Some days I add things, and other days I focus maybe one specific item. Either way, it is a daily practice that I have stuck to for years. I always feel a bit lighter and a bit more settled after I do my gratitude focusers.

May 2016

Sol loved the shoes and the jacket, which was a beautiful and smoky deep olive green, his favorite color. He'd been looking for one for a while now. His friends helped pick some of this stuff out. It was long overdue. The four of them were also long overdue for a friend reunion. It had been years since they were gathered like this.

The shoes were interesting. They had laces on the sides that help expand the shoe to provide a bit for more room for his wide feet. He took the clothing to the register to pay, but he couldn't find his Banana Republic card. He searched his wallet three times over, pulling everything out and putting it back in. Still, no luck.

The man in line behind him was getting angry at the long wait. Finally, the man tapped him rudely on the shoulder and said, "Are you going to hurry up and get this over with?" He looked at the man and felt a sudden rush of energy in his chest. He knew his body was telling him something based upon this interaction. He quickly realized that this was not a flight or fight situation, took a deep grounding exhaling breath, and said calmly, "Being angry is no way to go through life, sir." He finally found the card in his front pocket and paid for his clothes and left.

The interaction with the man made an impact for the day. He focused on treating people with respect and having patience for things that he couldn't control. He also focused on being present with his friends and not letting an outside influence affect him. When he focused on these things his anger, mostly driven by sadness and pain, dissolved as if watching a comet disappear into a black, starry sky.

THE WORK

Anger

Surviving the darker moments and the times that your anger, or your sadness or your grief, want to lead your way is absolutely possible. And you don't have to suffer as much. It is said that underlying most anger is indeed sadness or grief or unhealed trauma. Understanding this simple fact can in and of itself allow more grace to show up in your life for what you are experiencing currently or have gone through. There is a way to minimize the amount of time you are experiencing these negative emotions. The first is to feel it in your body. Our bodies don't lie. Do a quick body sensing exercise. Just sit and feel what's going on. Is your chest tight? That is one of my physical signs. Something that tells me to slow down for a minute. It is amazing what happens when you are able to do this. Once I do it, things don't seem as heavy or as serious anymore. I've become aware of what I am experiencing. It's become more objective to me. I can look at it from another angle.

At this point, and this is super important, do not trust or listen to any of your thoughts. Not a single one! It is said that a thousand thoughts can accompany a single emotion. This single emotion is that one that is ruining your life experience right now. But the moment you become aware of what is going on, now you have a choice! Now you can say, *OK, here's what I am feeling and here's what is going on. I can choose to feel like shit for as long as I want. I* can act like a baby and be miserable for hours. For days, for weeks, maybe even longer. Or I can choose to accept my situation and then drop the underlying emotions. You will find that it takes you only a few moments to get through these darker periods, where it used to take you much longer. Give yourself this gift and practice it daily.

August 1991

It seemed like it had been a long time since Sol last did a free-fall skydive with no tandem jumper or zip chord attached to the aircraft. In reality, it was only the day before when he did his first two jumps. No static line. No partner jumping. Just free falls by himself. How amazing.

This plane was different, though. It had two separate exit doors, one on each side of the aircraft. *How is this going to work?* Sol thought over the sound of the doors opening. He could feel the wind rushing in through the open jump door. His heartbeat started to increase, and his adrenaline was activating. Sol had trained for this for weeks and also felt confident at the same time.

The jumpmaster pointed at and mouthed for the first two jumpers to go to their respective doors. Sol knew that no matter how many jumps he'd done, there were still feelings of excitement and anxiousness as he would prepare to go. Out they went. It's said a good jump is when you can look back and see the jumpmaster waving at you as you begin your free fall. Sol stood at the door for his turn. Out he went, and after a few seconds he nailed a perfect arching posture and saw and waved back to the jumpmaster standing at the door of the plane. He fell weightlessly through the air for what felt like an eternity. Then, upon instinct, Sol opened his parachute and soaked up the experience and imagery as he floated like a leaf to the ground below. Sol experienced the concept of completely letting go of all fears and negative thoughts and reaped the benefits of doing so.

THE WAY

Beautiful Awareness

I love the idea of no self. Nothing to get hurt. Nothing to worry about. Nothing to fear. Nothing to attach to. Just presence. Just awareness, beautiful awareness. I just experienced this after my thirty-minute meditation today. My eyes were closed, and I was floating in an enormous, black empty field of awareness. When this happens, I can tap into the infinite possibility of my existence. Our field of awareness is indeed infinite, just like the universe. That is what I believe is meant when someone says God is inside of us or we are the universe. We are a microcosm of the great expanse. We are expansive inside. I know this because I have meditated on the concept of expansiveness for years. I have experienced what it feels like to be completely blissful in this state of meditation. It is during these moments that I can truly let go of everything. Let go of my anxiety from the day. Let go of my thoughts about tomorrow. Let go of trying to do anything at all. At this point of completely letting go, and in a sense giving up any and all effort, I experience beautiful awareness in its rawest form.

May 2003

Sol's son has been practicing this one for a while now. It's starting to sound more and more like the song itself. He's starting to play with other notes and tempos. It sounds good. "Nowhere Man" by the Beatles. He's on the porch. The windows to the house are open because the temperature dropped fifteen degrees today, bringing a coolness and breeze that has been much needed over the past month. The moment was perfect as he listened to his youngest son play and play and play. There was nothing else to do but sit, listen, be still, and enjoy these few moments.

Those moments of just sitting and being still never seem to last long enough, Sol thought as he ran from the field to the parking garage as the game was about to begin. A lacrosse stick always needs a bit of tweaking here and there, and this one, belonging to his son's teammate and friend, needed a new screw to keep the head on the shaft during the game. He volunteered to find a screwdriver and new screw for the stick. He left the field and unexpectedly found himself in the lower level of the garage. *Very confusing,* Sol thought, as now he found himself in a hospital room, which appeared to be an ER or ICU of some type. A ward for major cases.

Sol came upon a nurse who was working at her computer and asked for the tools division, as he needed a screwdriver. To his right was a man on a hospital bed who had lost both of his legs in some type of sporting accident. His nurse was asking him to say certain words while putting pressure down on what would be his lower extremities. But again, those weren't there. His insides were shown as a holograph on the wall across from his torso, and the nurse explained what was going on internally.

Sol ran back to the field just in time for the game to start. His son's team fixed his stick and then tossed the screwdriver onto the field by accident, causing the referee to throw a flag for unsportsmanlike conduct. Sol felt completely exhausted at this point, and he felt as if his body was trying to tell him something about the endless stream of thoughts that were overwhelming at the current moment. He wondered what he could do about stopping or controlling these unwanted thoughts.

THE WORK

Sit If You Need to Sit ...
Then Sit a Bit Longer

Meditation is simply about learning to recognize that you can slow your thoughts down, you can catch them before they grow, and that your thoughts come and go like clouds in the sky. They always pass. They don't have to have a tight hold on you. You don't have to attach to the thoughts and then create a story off them. You can recognize *Wow, I am having crazy thoughts right now*, and then let them pass and move on to the present moment.

These days, we don't rest as much as we need to. I'm referring to breaks in the day, not hours of sleep at night. These moments that we have to slow down a bit during the day to rest are so important. I typically use these moments to meditate or get a quick rest of my body and mind.

I experienced some amazing changes in my life when I started taking my daily meditation practices a bit more seriously. Yes, there are days where I don't want to meditate or do the work. It happens. However, I know the benefits of a consistent practice because I have been doing this for so long. This includes staying more consistent. Focusing on feelings and tying thoughts to those feelings to help rewrite a few of my internal stories. Joe Dispenza is very good at helping with this. Check out his meditations online if you're interested. I highly recommend it.

April 2024

Sol had walked through the halls of the financial services firm many times. This time was different, though. Although there were some familiar faces, there were also new ones as well, and people he hadn't seen for years. A few people he felt he had met, but mentally he was saying he didn't. He passed one of them making phone calls to prospective clients. He got to the end of the hall and entered the conference room.

These people Sol knew well, very well. They went through some basic computer steps, while he searched for his wrapped sandwich that he had bought at the local Soregel's deli a few hours before with his girlfriend. They both ordered the same thing, they usually do, and they love that. She loves the quinoa salad and pasta salad, this he knows.

As he parked his Volkswagen bug on the side of the one-way street, Sol noticed a man looking at him with intent. This man looked vaguely familiar. Ah, yes. He recalled that he wanted to hire one of his employees at one point in time. They talked business for a short time, and then the man left. Sol got back into his bug and turned the key in the ignition, but it wouldn't start. The car was old. He knew at some point soon he'd have to part ways with it. He got the car started and reparked, as the moving van had left the spots open when it departed. He sat in his car outside of this house. It was his place at one time. But things had changed now; everything was so different. Sol noticed the rest of his group ahead and walked toward them to meet for drinks. As he walked, he thought about the fact that none of the problems he just faced lasted forever, even though he felt like they would when they were happening. How cool.

Impermanence ... and Yes, What It Actually Means (LOL)

> The greater the doubt, the greater the awakening.
> The smaller the doubt, the smaller the awakening.
> —C.C. Change, *The Practice of Zen*

My body as I know it right now will die one day. And so will yours. The clouds that are floating across the morning sky as I write this will not last. The feeling of dread inside about an uncomfortable conversation or situation will not last. The feeling of an incredible piece of chocolate hitting your mouth and throat and body will not last either. Everyone and everything are in a process of growth and decay. The more I cling to wanting to live forever, the more suffering I will create for myself.

Impermanence is strongly linked to the process letting go as well as the concept of ownership. If we really want this amazing feeling of being able to weather the storms of life a bit better each day, then it is critical to think of things throughout your day that you may be holding on to but really need to let go. Letting go is the practice that will help you to understand and truly experience impermanence on a more frequent basis in your life. And we don't own these things that we need to let go of, either. I was in a past relationship where my partner really struggled with this one. She had a hard time of letting go of the fact that she didn't own me, and she struggled with letting things be as they imperfectly were. The result was a relationship that got suffocated into nothing. I forget if I read this or made this one up, but I love the analogy. If you squeeze a beautiful bird too lightly, it's either going to fly away or it will die. Everything is beautiful in life, and nothing is meant to be squeezed too tightly.

Understanding and experiencing impermanence is important for several reasons. First, it is a learned ability. You can learn, by practicing daily, to become less and less attached to—well, anything, really. It could be a material object such as your favorite car, your current work situation, the story in your head about you that seems to run daily through your mind. You know, the story you've had your whole life about your limitations, what's wrong with you, what you can't do, etc. And to bring it to a less dramatic level, it could even be the coffee you ordered this morning that didn't turn out the way you want it to turn out.

The sooner in each moment of life you can experience that nothing is permanent, you will be flying like a bird. Soaring away in life, doing what makes your heart happy and helps the most people. It's truly like some type of magic, in my opinion.

February 2018

Sol headed into his apartment for the night. As he came to his front door, his neighbor, who was also heading in for the night, stopped him for a moment. "Hey, your alarm clock woke me up this morning. It was that bird noise, and it went off at 5:00 a.m. And it I think your alarm clock is right up against my wall; at least it sounds like it." Sol apologized and told his neighborhood he would turn off the alarm, as he always got up before five anyway without the alarm. When he went into his bedroom, Sol couldn't find the alarm clock at first. Then he found it and pulled the plug out of the wall.

Sol's son was standing across the room. His eyes looked different, and his speech was off just enough for Sol to know something was going on. "Did you smoke weed just now?" he asked. His son nodded his head and walked toward the bedroom door. Sol lunged at his son, picked him up by the shirt, and pushed him against the wall. He looked into his eyes and ripped into him. His son's eyes teared up, and he said, "A dad should never say that to his son." His son left the room, leaving Sol there to ponder the words his son had just said to him. And they were exactly the same words that his own father would say to him growing up. Interesting how that chain is seldom broken. Sol wondered if he could indeed break some those chains that have been passed down from generation to generation, for the benefit of his children and their children.

THE WORK

Breaking the Chain

Nearly twelve years ago, I choose a life of sobriety because I needed to break the chain of the disease of alcoholism that has afflicted my family for decades. I am truly proud of myself for this breakthrough and commitment that allowed me to be fully present for my children. Being there for myself and facing reality head-on, especially throughout some very difficult times such as my divorce, has also increased my self-esteem and self-worth. Literally, I wouldn't be here today if I had gone back to drinking alcohol. I would not be writing this book. I would not have amazing relationships with my children. And most importantly, I wouldn't have a genuine relationship with myself based upon authenticity and self-trust. I don't think too much of where I might be or even if I'd be alive still if I were still drinking. There is a saying in Alcoholics Anonymous that goes, "Your next drink will kill you." Nothing could be truer for me and my journey through sobriety.

Some chains need to break with the hope to permanently change the behavior of future generations for the better as well as improve how one views oneself and treats others. I know that I am not perfect. I never will be and have stopped striving to be. I raise my voice at times with my children. I say things out of emotional reaction. I get defensive. However, I have never said the things that were said to me when I was growing up. Words can be so hurtful to young children, especially words from someone you trust and love. I prefer to lift up instead of putting down. I hope I am giving my children something positive to believe in, versus them doubting themselves and accepting their negative internal voice of doubt and low confidence.

What chains have you been wanting to break over the years? What areas of your own personal behavior are based upon past hurts and wounds from your childhood? It's never too late to flip that script. Once you have a year in of new behavior, it will feel good inside to say to yourself, *It's been a year since I .... I'm proud of you!*

October 1978

Sol debated which car to take. He wasn't sure about the weather. He chose the old blue Bonneville. Either choice was suboptimal at best, as both cars were outdated and dangerous, in his opinion. But they were his father's cars, and that's just how he rolled. As they hit the highway, the winds picked up, then the light snow. Sol felt OK at first, and then it happened.

The car was blown so hard by the wind that they slid sideways across the highway and into an embankment off the side of the rural road. They were not hurt, but certainly there were done for the day. They called the local group that is responsible for road accidents and then housing stranded motorists overnight at the inn. Sol's wife had decided to leave the baby with a friend and called someone to pick her up. She was drunk and pontificating about spiritual matters that she had no experience or knowledge of. He and his dad just shook their heads as they put her on speakerphone and let her rant away. They needed to pick up the baby soon, but they didn't know who this friend was who had his child.

Then the call came, and it was their turn to head home. They approached the drawbridge, and there were four options to choose from, none of which led to where they wanted to go. Sol had to get home, though, so he picked the one that sounded best. West Donnington is where they headed. Sol decided at this moment that he was going to pay more attention to what his intuition was trying to tell him about relationships and situations. He had a deep desire to depend less on outside circumstances and more on himself.

Discovering Your Inner Light

Don't get me wrong. I am an avid learner and reader, and I don't think that will ever change in my lifetime. However, there are times when I think to myself, *How many spiritual books do I need to read to feel OK? What do I keep looking for? Am I looking for progress or a solution? I've read all the answers. Do I think there's another answer in another book? And then another answer in another book? And then another answer in another book? When does it end? When do I stop? When do I slow down and enjoy myself? My progress? My experience, without trying to make it better?* Reading more and more was just veiling me from my life. So, I finally decided to take my writing more seriously.

As I write this book, I am overwhelmed with the feeling of joy for creating something from the inner space that I have worked so very hard to get back to. I am honored and grateful to be able to share my wisdom and help other people with what I know, what I have experienced, and what I have learned. To share my gift, because I have so much to give. If I'm reading, I'm not giving. I'm trying to get more. I don't need more. I need less. I need to strip down and give more. Create more. Be more. And not be as in being a better person. I know I am good person. I want to be more content and grateful, truly appreciate what I have, what I have learned, and what I have been through. Appreciate each moment, instead of worrying or trying to read something to make things better. Things are already better; I am just masking it with my seeking.

This book is about stopping the seeking. Stopping the grasping. Stopping the running. Stopping the worry. This book is about coming home to who I am. Rediscovering the power of the pure love that is inside me, the power of my own light. Not the light of someone else who has written a book. The light inside me. The light that I have always had. Not watching another series on TV. Creating something from the love and light that is me. I am love. I am light. I am.

Time to share. Time to stop being greedy. Time to stop being a spender and a taker. Time to be a creator and a sharer. Time is running out. The time is now. The time is always now. There is no other time. Time to start my life's work. Time to give back. Time to stop collecting books and spending more and wasting my time. Time to create. Time to take it seriously, but not too seriously. Every time I want to buy a book, or read a current book, or watch a show—I will create instead. I will do tai chi, play the piano, write, or draw. I am creation. You are creation. We are all creation.

March 2020

Sol hadn't seen most of these people since graduating from the Air Force Academy, and some even longer, back in high school. Wow, thirty years ago. The restaurant was crowded, and they all knew each other in some way or another. The drinks were flowing, and the moods were high. Most were sitting in the same groups that they ran with back in the day. Sol stopped by various tables and chatted with some of them. He still could not make sense of why everyone was gathered on this evening.

One guy named Mike was from the academy and hadn't changed much at all. The same Texas drawl. The same face and beaming smile. He tended to try to be on the hard-ass side at the academy, but he seemed to have softened a bit as he aged. Amazing what life and experience can do to someone when it comes to personality and approach. They say people don't change. Sol thinks that is both true and not true. Most of them here had not changed much at all, yet they were all different in some way or another.

People Can Change (It's Just That You Can't Change Them)

I'm sure you've heard it a thousand times, and probably have said it a hundred. "People don't change." It was said to me many times during my marriage, and it made me feel boxed in, constricted, and devalued. Looking back now, I can understand why I was told that, as she was talking from a place of fear. "People don't change" needs to be broken down and analyzed a bit more to truly understand. I am a person, and I have changed. I have put in years and years of doing work on myself, and I have changed.

Now, that being said, I do often wonder if I have actually changed, or have I rediscovered who I was before I was programmed by parents, growing up, society, etc.? In other words, when you truly flip the script and shed your old story, have you changed, or have you become who you really were again, which is more centered around pure love and connection? I believe it to be both, and that to me is such a beautiful thing.

During my journey to reconnect with my true self, there were times when I found myself subconsciously digging my feet in and not allowing the change to happen. It was at those times that I felt a very strong invisible force was keeping me from changing. Call it ego or whatever, it was very strong. Through my meditation practice, I have picked up the skill of detecting my thoughts early in the development process. When I sense this thought or feeling coming on, I almost get a bit excited now and say to myself, *Bring it on, ego, you don't want me to revert because you are comfortable with how I've been the past thirty years*. It's like a challenge to me and I fully accept the challenge. I have directly experienced pure love and enlightenment many times, so it's an easy challenge for me now to accept the slight stubbornness to change, and then do it anyway!

Please do not ever give up on yourself. Ever. There is always a way. Go find it. Do the *work* and you will find the *way*.

September 2010

Sol couldn't believe it was him. He saw the name on the agenda earlier in the day, but he tossed it aside as coincidence. Yet there he was, right in front of him, sitting down at the conference table preparing to speak for the next few hours. They made eye contact, and he sent a sly smile Sol's way. They last saw each other playing together on the high school soccer team. No, wait. It was a twenty-year high school reunion. As he sat down at the table, the speaker smiled and said to him, "Can I just give you the handouts and call it day?" in a joking way. He wasn't sure why his friend didn't want to give the talk now. As they took a break midway through the meeting, they gathered in the back of the room. A woman walked by and handed out masks to protect from COVID. Really, this is still going on? Sol looked over to the right, and someone had let their small dog into the conference room. They were chasing him down and having fun with it. A much-needed break from the serious discussion at hand.

After the conference, Sol understood what was going on. His friend had gotten the call a few minutes prior to giving his talk letting him know that his wife just passed. After the call, his friend collapsed in Sol's arms and was crying uncontrollably. His family was off to the side huddled together, also crying uncontrollably. The death was sudden and unexpected. She was too young, as is often said when someone passes away before their time. But Sol had to work that day, as he was on set, and they were filming a scene with him as Willy Loman in *Death of Salesman*. After makeup, Sol was unrecognizable and played the part perfectly. He now understood why his friend did not want to present publicly that day. Afterward, Sol was overcome by an immense feeling of how precious life really is, and how you just never know what can happen in life. He vowed to keep this mind more often.

THE WORK

Live Each Day as If It Were Your Last

Why do we always strive so hard for something? To earn the extra bonus at work. To buy a nicer car. To get that bigger home. There's always something next. I've played and coached lacrosse for the past thirty-five years. It is a such a beautiful sport. It's called the creator's game. I made All-State in Pennsylvania in high school. But I wasn't satisfied, because Scott made All-American. I started every game for four years for a Division One college program and was cocaptain of the team my senior year. But I didn't score enough goals, didn't make All-American, didn't make the North-South game.

I never played professionally. All disappointments for me. Yet when I coach these youth teams, there is so much beauty in the game. So many cool creations that occur on the field, at an individual level, a team level, and a competition level. It's so awesome. My college coaches just wanted me to be satisfied and content with my level of play. They said I amazed them at times and was so fun to watch. I created an experience for them and myself. I did amazing things on the field with the stick, ball, my feet, and my teammates. Yet, I wasn't satisfied. Why aren't we satisfied? Why do we need more of everything? What's it all for if we're not content, enjoying it? Why do we have to wait for the rain to stop to be happy? Why can't we just enjoy the rain. It's so beautiful, so

44

creative, so life-giving. Did you ever just listen to the rain? I mean really listen to the rain. It has so much to say. It's a miracle when you think about it.

I now know that each day I get to wake up healthy is a gift. There is no guarantee of a tomorrow. My manifestation meditations have changed how I view each day when I wake, and that was by intent. I no longer wake up with angst or dreading what I may have to face that day. If I do, I am able to quickly change my view before I get out of bed. At one point in my life, I was used to waking up with those negative feelings. It was almost a habit, sad to say. I always felt that there had to be a better way, and I often didn't understand why I felt that way. There's a saying in the Adult Children of Alcoholics world that describes the concept of living in chaos and then getting used to living in that chaos. It took me a long time and I did a lot of this work to understand how that was manifesting in my life. Finally, I got sick and tired of feeling sick and tired, and I realized if I truly loved myself, I would treat myself better each morning and not put myself through that angst, if possible. Fortunately, it is possible to flip that script. I am so grateful for my mornings now, and I give thanks to God and the universe for each additional one I get.

July 1987

Sol was stuck on the roof, and he didn't know how he was going to get down. He was on the very top of a pointed roof, where his friend had just made a leap toward safety that would have been difficult to believe if he hadn't seen it with his own eyes. Sol wasn't sure how he was going to pull it off. There was no easy way down. He felt his foot slip and grabbed tighter onto the overhang. Finally, he took the step and jumped down to his right, where he handed safely on a small platform that led him inside.

When he got downstairs, Sol joined his two friends, and the

three of them gathered at a table and discussed music and a recent album that they collaborated on. After that, he met friends at the inside sports arena, where they played soccer with a huge blown-up light ball. The ball would curve in crazy ways if you kicked it hard enough. The teams were fluid, and there were many games going on at the same time in the sports complex that housed five soccer fields inside.

After the games ended, Sol departed the stadium to head home. On the way to his car, he saw him, and he made a split decision to approach him. He was face-to-face with him, and he was at least six inches shorter than he was. He hadn't seen him since the incident with his ex-wife in his house years ago. It brought up a lot of strong, negative emotions. He took at the swing at the big man, who caught his arm and locked it up. They started to wrestle a bit, and then a bystander caught the encounter on video. The video was posted on the internet and became somewhat of a funny meme for a bit. After that, the bystander called the police on the two of them. Sol followed the police and interrogators to the small, one-floored white building. His intent was to eavesdrop on the interrogations. He wasn't sure what he would hear, or why he cared. He sneaked around the outside of the building and hid next to each window, listening intently for any pieces of juicy information.

Suddenly, he heard a constant white-noise sound that was not allowing him to hear the interrogations anymore. He went to the other side of white building and saw someone in one of the windows. Sol approached the window and saw that it was his old college buddy, who was feeding feed to the chickens in the yard. He asked his friend to stop so that he could hear the interrogations. His friend did stop, and then joined Sol in the eavesdropping fun. Sol was amazed at how the experience had instantly seem to flip from seriousness to joy when he spotted his college buddy feeding the chickens. He decided to stay with joy during the experience for as long as possible.

THE WAY

Choose Joy, Because Why Not?

It's a Monday afternoon, and I worked hard today. I'm doing the right things. I'm taking responsibility. I'm responding to what each situation demands, with the intention of not making it about me. It really is truly freeing. I'm outside on the front porch, reading a bit more about karma. I love to sit out here. I miss this in the wintertime, and it was a long winter that makes me appreciate being out here that much more. Sometimes I just listen when I sit out here. Sometimes I just look. Sometimes I battle the thoughts that I'm wasting my time out here. Sometimes I think this is happiness, that it's as simple as sitting outside in nature and being and observing.

We strive so much. What's the endgame? Why do we feel like failures when we take time to sit outside and observe? There's a leaf blower in the neighborhood. There always seems to be one every day at this time of year. It's midspring. A mom jogs up the sidewalk while her young son rides his bike. My neighbor pulls into his driveway, stops part way up, and walks down to his mailbox. A routine he does every day. My sons are inside putting do-rags on their heads. The sun is popping out of the clouds every now and then, and the birds are still talking to each other. The clouds are barely moving, like a slow creep across the sky. The wind chimes that my daughter gave me for Christmas a few years ago make a beautiful light sound in the breeze. Houses are selling fast in the neighborhood.

I considered a move back to West Chester, the town outside of Philadelphia where I grew up. It's been over six years since I moved out here to Pittsburgh. School bus number ninety-six drives down the street, bringing the elementary kids home to their parents. Remote learning at school is slowly becoming a thing of the past. But the kids are still wearing masks on the bus.

I'm two weeks out of a long-term relationship. It's been many, many years since I've been on my own. A counselor told me when I was going through my divorce that I need to create relationships where I don't need anything from the other person. That's powerful stuff. It is said that is not what you do, but how you do what you do. I am making dinner for the boys right now, and I am doing it with joy inside. Why not? Why be miserable and moody and look at it like a chore? Why not celebrate the opportunity and be grateful that I can serve and nourish them, enabling them to literally live another day? How lucky I am, truly.

December 2002

Sol entered his living room, and the boy and his uncle were sitting on the far left of the couch. He didn't recognize either of them or most of the people in his house this day. Something felt off, so he watched the boy for a few minutes as he strolled the room. And then, the boy pulled out a bowl and lit up some weed. Right in the living room with the all the people! The boy could not have been older than fifteen. The uncle just sat there as if nothing was wrong. *Maybe the boy has a medical condition, and the weed is prescribed medicine*, Sol thought. He told the boy that he couldn't do that in here, and the boy said, "Why not?" Well, for starters, it's illegal. And second, I don't want anyone smoking weed in my house. The boy still would not listen, so Sol walked over and grabbed the bowl out of the boy's hand. The uncle was not very happy about this.

Sol left the house and went out back where his two sons were hitting golf balls. They had asked him to join them earlier, but he couldn't. They asked him if he could hit a golf ball up that hill and over that house. "Sure, no problem, boys," he said, knowing it wasn't the right thing to do because he could accidently hit a house. Sol took out his trusted six iron, placed the ball nicely up on a piece of grass so as to give himself a nice lie, and slowly swung a perfectly timed golf shot. The club hit the ball perfectly, and the ball flew up the hill and over the house in front of them. They all just smiled at each other.

Then he heard the screeching tires. The two pickup trucks were moving way too fast for these crowded streets in the small town. The big blue one jumped the curb and was heading down one alleyway at about forty miles per hour. The other smaller red truck stayed to the right and headed down a parallel alley. They were definitely chasing someone or something. People jumped out of the way to avoid being nailed by the speeding trucks. A few moments later, a group of girls on their bikes were escorting a young boy on his bike, as if they were flying in front of him in formation à la the Blue Angels. Yes, this is what the trucks were chasing, and it looks like the boy is safe, for now. For a brief few moments, Sol pondered the situation and understood how important feeling safe is and how the definition of safe can change depending upon the situation and the people involved.

THE WORK

Safety

In high school or college, many of us learned from Maslow's hierarchy of needs that safety is one of our most fundamental needs. What does "safe" mean to you? Is it physical safety from the harm of others? Is it safety from an emotional standpoint of just being a human being on this spinning ball of energy? Is it safety in relationships with other people, hoping you will never get hurt again?

For me, it was all of the above for many years. I firmly believe that we cannot expand into who we truly are until safety issues are understood and dealt with at a profound level within. I can say that I feel safe now. And if you knew about all what I've been through, you'd be amazed, actually. I'm sure I'd feel the same way about you. If you don't feel safe, you cannot be your authentic self in situations. You will be in a defensive posture. You won't be able to listen to others clearly. You will shut others out of your life. You could potentially ruin really good relationships.

A good analogy to help here is thinking about your inner child, the younger version of you, that created anxiety and stress reactions with the goal of coping with perceived dangers and with feeling unsafe. If you can stay mindful when you feel unsafe, you will notice that your inner child is reacting as if you were still living in the past, as a younger, more vulnerable person. Your inner child does not want to lose his or her job of protecting you, as they have been doing it your whole life. And for a time during your younger years, it was incredibly helpful and critical to your survival. Help your inner child understand that there is nothing in your outer world causing you real harm, at least in most of your life situations. All the things that we view are unsafe are literally made up inside of us due to years and years of programming and habitual behavior patterns. We are literally addicted to these feelings sometimes. Once you understand, through meditation and the way, that you are in control of what is safe and what is not, you will see a noticeable difference in your stress levels throughout your day.

Take some time to understand what safety means to you. Go back and study Maslow's pyramid for a few minutes if you need to learn a bit more about the definition of safety. Then meditate on safety. Journal about it. You will be absolutely thrilled with the results.

April 2001

Sol looked at the hotel phone for a third time. He had hung up on her a few minutes earlier. He didn't want to take the incoming call again. He was away on business, as was often the case these days. He bought her a mug and tea kit for her birthday, and she mocked the gifts a few moments ago. He hung up because he was hurt. He had tried his hardest to buy a nice gift, but it was never his strong suit. Sol headed out to meet his team and forgot about the phone call and the gift.

The game was a combination of lacrosse, golf, and indoor soccer, and it is played in an indoor arena while holding a football. The goal was to throw the football into the net. The boys were playing hard that day. Brad, who was one of Sol's teammates and good friends, came around the side but just couldn't get the shot off in time. They were cheering him on to turn the other way, as the goal was wide open. Being one of the slower players on the team, Brad tried but couldn't pull off the shot. The ball turned over, and the opposing team took it down and scored quite easily. The score was 1–6, and they were getting trounced, but Sol was enjoying himself as always and looked forward to moving on to the golf part of the event.

The course looked vaguely familiar, but Sol couldn't find the tee box. He looked around in all directions. *This couldn't be where I tee off from, or could it be?* Sol thought to himself. There were trees directly in front of him, as well as to the left and right. A voice from behind pointed Sol further to the left of where he was looking. There they were, the white tees. Sol approached the tee box and noticed there was a white tent on top of it, covering the entire area. He went under the tent and tried a back swing with his driver. The driver hit the top of the tent on his backswing. This wasn't going to work.

Sol went back into his bag, and grabbed a tiny club with a driver's head, but only about a foot long. He swung and topped the ball about thirty-five yards in front of him to the left of the fairway, into the rough. This would have to do for now. He walked into the clubhouse where the pro asked him if there was bad weather out there. The golf pro said no, but Sol needed some food before continuing his round. The pro gave him a juice box container that had beef broth and meat chunks inside it, and Sol downed the box of liquid quickly. Apparently, it was all the rage on the golf course these days. Off he went to finish off his game. As he continued with his golf game, the beauty of the scenery and the course design began to take over his experience. He was in awe of the rolling fairways and how they magically shifted into the rough and tall brown grass blowing in the wind. The colors seemed magical, and he really had no words to describe the experience, even if he tried to.

THE WORK

Standing in the Rain with No Labels

Communicating clearly and with intent can be so difficult sometimes, especially when uncomfortable emotions are involved. My son Sean and I just had a nice discussion this morning and he said to me, "I wish I could be the monkey from *Cloudy with a Chance of Meatballs*, and all I had to do was think and the other person would understand." After he walked away, I contemplated what he had said for the next few minutes.

What's that word I am looking for when I am walking Finn, my three-and-a-half-year-old rottweiler, down the street at six-thirty on a Saturday morning in midspring? The neighborhood is blessed with the sound of the birds, but that's about it for this morning. But what's that word when you feel that everything is OK, and you don't need anything right now in this very moment. There's nothing to strive for, nothing to improve upon, and there's nothing else that needs to be done in this moment. Is it peace? Joy? Grace? Happiness? Contentment? Appreciation? Acceptance? And to go one step further, does the label even matter? Do I need it to properly address the experience, or is it good enough to simply feel the experience without the label? After all, it was a beautiful experience this morning. Beautiful! I just had to name it, I guess.

We don't close our eyes enough and just listen to the rain. And God forbid, simply stand in the rain and get wet on purpose! I took

Finn out this morning, and I just stood in the light rain while he did his thing. I felt wonderful, refreshed, and energized simply by standing in the rain and doing nothing at all. Why don't we do it more? What's our problem with just slowing down? It's Monday morning, gotta run, run, run and do, do, do.

Part of the way is to become more aware of times that you feel you are rushing around frantically and wearing yourself down. Take care of yourself. Listen to your body. We, as human beings, are not designed to be on the go continuously. We need breaks. Physical breaks, mental breaks, emotional breaks. When I truly accepted the fact that I need rest daily, I began to have more energy each day. My body needs rest and my mind needs rest. When I lie down for a twenty-minute nap, I say to myself, *I am resting my mind and body.*

My girlfriend bought me a book titled *The Drummer and the Great Mountain—A Guidebook to Transforming Adult ADD/ADHD* by Michael Joseph Ferguson. ADD has played this crazy dance with me since I was a young boy. Sadly, like most other boys and girls, I never had a diagnosis or counseling for it in middle and high school. Ferguson does an amazing job of helping us understand the link between hunting and farming, or in our day and age it's called work and rest. When humans hunted back in the day for food, they didn't hunt from nine to five for eight hours five days a week. They hunted hard, and then rested. Hunted again, and then rested. If you struggle with ADHD/ADD, I highly recommend Ferguson's book. It has transformed my life, and I am forever grateful for the gift my girlfriend gave me that day.

March 2011

They had to escape. So, they packed all their essentials in black garbage bags. They opened the door to the hallway, looked both ways, and saw that the coast was clear. They quickly headed through the door across the hallway and up the stairs to exit the building. It was dark outside but getting lighter by the minute. They didn't have much time to spare. Sol opened the door, and as he did, he noticed there was someone walking to their car. The female got in her own car and drove away. Phew. That was too close for comfort, and fortunately she did not see them at the doorway. They headed to the escape pod. Another car appeared just seconds later, and Sol swears he saw the younger passenger make eye contact. But they left as well, again not noticing them hiding near the pod. They opened the hatch to the pod. It was a semicircular craft with seating around the outside walls. They quickly brought their belongings in and got ready for departure.

She left her toothbrush on the counter. Sol was in the middle of brushing his teeth, and she looked at him with a look that said I'm proud of you but I don't trust you at the same time. But she seemed happy and pleased. Sol finished brushing his teeth and let her know that her toothbrush was in there still. He was getting ready for a party where his daughter would be singing and playing guitar with a new band at an outside concert. Sol felt excited and nervous at the same time, as this was the first time he'd see her perform with this group. He knew she would do well, as she excels at almost everything she does.

Sol met up with some old work buddies, and they talked shop and about how each of them were chasing after the next big sale in finance. They shared ideas, although Sol wasn't in that business anymore. He had moved on years ago to pursue something that more aligned with who he was inside. Even though he left that career, he didn't give up on himself or his family. Sol persevered, knowing that others were depending upon him to show up for life and do the right thing.

THE WAY

Don't Walk Out

I took my son Sean, my middle child, to the movies. He must have been around eight or nine years old. I wasn't feeling great emotionally or mentally before we went to the movies, and I almost didn't take him at all. It was one of those feelings inside that I know how to describe only as a sticky sensation that just won't leave my body or mind. Pema Chodron has a wonderful way of describing this feeling, which she calls "shenpa." Pema reminds us not to scratch the itch; just let it be, and it will pass much faster. To this day, I can sense when my shenpa is popping its head up inside of me, but now I am much better at letting it speed right through my being and not stay too long.

I wanted to see how I would feel later, after the movies. Would it change this feeling inside? As we got back home from the movies, I couldn't believe how much better I felt emotionally and mentally. I almost felt like a completely different person than before the movie … and it had only been a few hours of time! The movie was the perfect one to see with Sean. *Rango* was a comic movie for kids, and the storyline was fantastic. Clint Eastwood showed up at the end and said, "No man can walk out on his story." That was pretty powerful to me. I was not going to walk out on myself. Leave myself stranded not feeling any better in life. Was not going to give up. What an amazing surprise message to receive through this movie.

The movie (although comic) also talked about the meaning of life, who we are, and having courage in the face of difficulty.

September 2022

Sol hadn't seen Tony in months, let alone spent any quality time together with him. They headed up the windy back roads toward the restaurant, yet something seemed off with Tony. He was driving, and the car started drifting off into a neighborhood yard. Sol turned his head and said, "Hey, Tony. Everything OK, man?" Tony replied that everything was fine. Sol thought to himself it was fine; it was just Tony being Tony. They let another car pass, an older woman out for a night drive. They arrived at the restaurant and waited for the hostess to take their name and seat them. The place was crowded that night, a nice buzz of conversation in the air. Sol helped the old woman at the hostess table who was standing in front of them. She couldn't find her keys. They looked around for their table, as the hostess seemed to have let them choose their own seating area. They discussed sitting outside, but it was too cold that night. They found a nice community table among a larger group of people and enjoyed an amazing dinner together with meaningful conversation.

On the way home, Tony wanted to take the wheel again, although he had too many drinks to be driving them home. The rental car was a Jeep Cherokee, a newer model. Before they got in the car to leave, another family with two young children were walking behind them. They had a dog, a tiny, tiny dog that would roll over and lie on its back and beg for treats. It was really cute, even though Sol was not a small dog person. They headed out on the road, and once again Tony was swerving on the road. It was extremely dark outside; the roads were mostly downhill, and the weather was getting bad. Sol felt completely uneasy and had a lot of anxiety about the situation. They stopped at the bottom of the next hill, and switched seats so Sol could take the wheel and drive them both home safely. That made him feel much better. Sol was relieved that he had done the right thing. He knew that doing the right thing as often as possible would allow him to be there for himself and his children to the best extent possible.

THE WAY

On Being a Single Dad

Being a single father has been a bit of a juxtaposition to me. What I mean by that is that you have to put your children first. But to put your children first, you have to put yourself first. Sounds crazy, doesn't it? If you have flown in an aircraft at any point in your life, you have heard the flight attendant instruct the passengers that in the event of an emergency, you are to put your own air bag on first and then help others. The theory is that you can't help someone else if you can't breathe. Where I struggled at times being a single dad is I wanted to put their oxygen masks on first. I'd easily take a bullet for any one of my three children if it came down to it. Easily. But this was different from that. It was a difficult lesson for me to learn, and it was often taught to me through my children.

You can't help your children if you're not healthy, if you're not stable, and especially if you're not aware of your thoughts and emotions and how your reactions impact your children. If you don't know yourself very well. And certainly, if you don't feel good about yourself inside each morning when you wake up and each night when you go to sleep. You are setting an example for your children. Whether you know or not, and whether you like it or not, you are a role model. Your children watch everything you do. They take mental notes. They absorb shit. Remember, when they are grown adults, they are bringing filters into their human experience, many

59

of which were put in place by you. That's right. Another piece of irony—we are very powerful as parents and at the same time mostly powerless.

Here's an example of what I mean when I say that you need to take care of yourself first. Sobriety is extremely important to me. It's a major dragon I slayed over twelve years ago. I started drinking alcohol at the age of thirteen. The first time I drank it was Jack Daniels, and I got drunk and quickly discovered both the very highs and the very lows of the effects of alcohol on me personally. To this day, I still wince at the smell of Jack Daniels.

Alcohol was my method of self-medicating during a traumatic period during middle and high school, although I didn't know that was what I was doing at the time. It just made me feel better and forget about pain and sorrow of my current situation. And sadly, no one stepped in to help me navigate the mess I was slowly creating for myself. My parents were struggling with their own addictions and didn't have the time, ability, or resources to help me with mine. While I took a five-year break in my early twenties from alcohol, it continued to play the ineffective role of self-medication for me into my late thirties. I had many situations where I didn't treat others properly and where I had near misses with death. To this day, I am certain God and the universe carried me through those days of blindness and suffering.

I was four years into my sobriety when my then wife told me that she wanted a divorce. There's a lot of truth behind the statement that relationships change when an alcoholic achieves sobriety. Four years may sound like a lot of time, but those of you who have been there you know that it takes a shit ton of diligence to stay on your path. There has not been a single moment over the past eight years that I thought about having a drink of alcohol. I've had some really weird and interesting dreams about it, and some of those you are reading in this very book through Sol. I once told a therapist that I couldn't live if I knew that I couldn't drink alcohol. Now, it's the opposite. I can't imagine living with alcohol. I am not telling you to stop drinking alcohol. However, if it is interfering with your ability to parent properly, including holding a job, then absolutely get help as soon as possible. Life is too short and precious to waste your time away.

If I started drinking again during that time, I wouldn't be here right now. Not sure where I would be, but it wouldn't be in a good place at all. That's what I mean when I say that you have to take care of yourself first. Maintaining my sobriety through the early stages of the shit show we call divorce was crucial for me. It kept me clear-headed. I never woke up feeling like shit or beating myself up for tying one on again the night before. I didn't fall into that endless cycle of numbing my feelings and then feeling like shit both mentally and physically for numbing my feelings. Instead, I woke up well rested each morning, and then I meditated daily. Sleep is so important. I maintained a super healthy weight. Again, all these things added up to taking care of myself and feeling great inside for it.

One last note. I talk about being a single dad because I am a man. The same can be said of single moms, as we are all in this human experience together. I have so much respect for both single dads and single moms. It truly is one of the most challenging and rewarding undertakings of my life.

June 1998

The flight out of Pittsburgh was at first just delayed a few hours. Then it was moved to tomorrow. Then all flights were shifted to fly out of Cleveland in a few days, instead of Pittsburgh. Sol looked out the airport window; the sky was clear. There were no storms around, so he wondered what was going on. He had tickets for his kids but needed them to be there when he spoke with the terminal agent to get updated tickets. The two men behind the United counter were handling baggage and pointed him to the upstairs kiosks, where his change in travel plans could be properly taken care of. Sol headed upstairs to get everything straightened out.

When he arrived at his destination, they presented Sol with a box, and inside that box was a certificate of achievement. Sol felt proud as he'd been serving the military for eight years now. He also found a check for ninety dollars from one of his favorite airmen on his team of enlisted personnel. This was a lot of money from an airman who was making very little and supporting a wife and three children. That gesture was the most important and heartfelt experience he had so far during this process. Finally, they pinned his jump wings on his uniform, signifying that he had successfully completed free fall parachute school. Does he ever want to get back in a plane again, knowing he would jump out? Not a chance in hell.

On the flight home, Sol was seated toward the back of the aircraft, yet it didn't feel like your typical airplane. All of a sudden, the plane went into the first turn and the right wing dipped very low, too low for an airliner, indeed. Sol was OK, but it did feel a bit steep. A few minutes later, another turn. This one, however, ended up in two full spins. *How did that just happen?* Sol thought. An airliner with passengers on board doing full spins! As the passengers left the plane and walked down the hall, one of them said, "Maybe the plane didn't spin! Maybe they just spin the cabin!" This really made him think. *Is that possible? And if it is, what else in life is happening like that where he thought he knew the truth, but didn't?*

Sol met his friend in the outdoor seating area in the middle of the condominium complex. It had started to rain, so they found a dry spot. Their other friend was above in the one of the balconies, shouting down to them. He wanted to know if they had plans for the day, and if not, if they would go with him to volunteer to help coach boys' lacrosse. Of course, they all said yes.

At this moment, Sol understood the importance of staying open to other experiences and keeping his heart open to other people and himself. He felt that this was one of the secrets to finding purpose in his life.

THE WORK

Stay Open to New Paths

I love food. Absolutely love it. All kinds at any time is my motto! The problem was that no matter how hard and long I worked out, I couldn't lose about ten pounds of fat around my belly and love handles. It definitely felt like a car tire on that part of my body, and it was bringing me down. I wasn't feeling good about myself because I knew exactly what I needed to do to change the situation. The extra weight was making runs harder than they needed to be. The quick glances in the mirror after showers was depressing me. I didn't like it. I would do intermittent fasting here and there, but I found that I would run out of energy in the early evening, say between four and six o'clock.

So, intermittent fasting was helping a bit as far as shedding a few pounds here and there, but it was not helping from an energy standpoint. I am a big believer in staying awake in life to accept situations that are given to me by the universe to help me be a better man and person and enjoy life to the fullest. So, when my buddy Mags from the Air Force Academy let me know that he was going to be traveling down from Boston for his son's hockey tournament, I of course said yes to meeting him for food and his son's game, as we have often done since this first time.

This get-together was life changing in a few ways. First off, we hadn't seen each other since we worked together at Andrews Air

Force Base in Maryland. Maybe once after that at the most, so it was good for my soul to hang out and catch up on shit and family stuff. The other thing that happened was that Mags told me he had lost a ton of weight recently. I asked how, and he said that he and his wife were doing Whole30. And once he told me that he lost weight in his armpits (no joke!), I was thinking, *How do I start?* I love learning about new things. Always have.

I dived in right in as I often do when I'm excited about a new way to help myself become better and live life more fully. Notice above that I didn't say Whole30 diet, and that was on purpose. It's more of a lifestyle for me personally at this point. And it's not about being too restrictive or not enjoying food. In fact, the opposite has happened. It has gotten me back to cooking more, which I love and have missed. I was eating more calories and healthier food and losing weight. See, it's all these little things that come to you in life, if you're open to them and say yes, that help you take care of yourself better. The universe is abundant and generous and smart, if you are able to pick up what it's putting down!

I've since lost the ten pounds of belly fat including three belt loops, and I had to get a new belt and new jeans! I am at a weight and body fat percentage that is more ideal for me. I feel healthy at a very raw and natural level. Like this is how I am supposed to be. I don't obsess over my weight as much as I used to. And I'm not on the scale weighing myself every day anymore; I simply go by how I feel. More on measurement later—in all aspects of life. Listen, Whole30 is not for everyone. I understand that. I am not getting paid by them for this either. It's just what has worked really well for me personally, with amazing effects. It takes discipline and effort to make it work. But like in all areas of life, once you have the process down it becomes more effortless, and you start to enjoy the smaller things in life that can be so fulfilling—like the smell of a butternut squash soup hot on the stove or the sweetness contained in a simple strawberry. Hmm, I didn't really need huge party-sized M&M bags in my office after all. I thought I did, but it was just mindless hand grabbing and comfort eating that was going against what I really wanted.

May 1994

Sol couldn't find his lacrosse gloves or stick anywhere on the sideline. Where did he put his stuff this time? He'd been selected to play on the All-USA lacrosse team, but when his big moment came, he wasn't ready. Someone found his stuff on the sideline, and Sol geared up and ran into the game, but only after his team got a penalty for him being on the field late. On the field, Sol felt slow, too slow. Something didn't feel right. It took him twice as long to run down toward the end of the field, which seemed miles away. The game was happening, and Sol was on the field, but he couldn't get close enough to participate and have an impact on the game. He was in his own way now, thinking about what he was afraid of, like not meeting the expectations that he feels others have placed on him. It could be that he has set himself unreasonable standards that he thinks he needs to achieve in order to be noticed and appreciated by other people in daily life.

After the game, Sol saw the group gathering down the hill at the intersection of the two roads. The three of them felt like they were on an adventure, and they were to some extent, they just didn't know the half of it yet. An interesting thing happened as they neared the group of college students. The college students all scattered at the last minute, except for the group leader. And when the three of them joined the leader, the others quickly came back. Each one of them had a unique facial disfiguration, from skin color to scars to sunken eyes.

They entered the laboratory room and were strapped into standing gurneys that made a large circle around the room. The wires and lines were connected, and every piece of internal body information was being recorded. Sol's didn't have the main strap that was used to begin the process, so his leader had to go find one. As that was happening, one of the students running the experiment threw up all over the floor, with cigarettes and beer coming out. Apparently, he had had a rough night, and what he put into his body was not jiving with the experiment requirements. Sol looked over at his friend Jay, and they exchanged glances. Jay was trying to apply himself to the experiment to get the most out of the experience, but something was bothering him.

Sol realized that during the lacrosse game he placed way too much importance on how he was doing, and not enough importance on what he was doing. He reminded himself to pay more attention to form and process going forward, and less attention to the actual results.

Careful How You Measure You

I have learned that it is very important to not obsessively measure myself on how I am doing as a human being on this spinning ball of energy. The problem is, we tend to measure—well, almost everything! For example, I go on a run, and I continue to think about my pace. How fast am I running? I used to measure every run, and my results tended to dictate whether I was happy afterward. I ran 8.75 miles on the morning of writing this section of the book, and I was not happy with my pace! What the heck is going on? I eat a large dinner, and I wonder how much I weigh. So, I weigh myself every day. And I get upset or am happy at the results. I'm at an amazing weight right now, and if I go up a pound or two, I get upset! What is going on here? Did it start in school when we were always measured on everything we did? What was my grade? Did I pass, fail, nail it, slide on by?

If I don't want my mood to be driven by something outside of myself, then what's the alternative? How about instead of measuring results, we focus on form and process and enjoyment? The same can be said about myself when I think of myself as a single dad. It's OK to check in with yourself occasionally to make sure you're not missing any major rocks. At the same time, you need to give yourself a break daily. Don't measure or compare yourself to anyone. A friend recently told me something interesting that he said to his son. He said, "Be a good person, be kind and work hard, and you will be OK no matter what career path you take." What great advice! So, I can do the same as a single dad. Be the best person, best man, best role model I can be for my children. Do things, say things, and act so that in five or ten or fifteen years you will hear your children say how important you were to them during this difficult time for them. Remember, you are a role model for sure!

October 2014

Once the summer ends, the vacationers leave, and the locals stay put or return back here. Money is not spent as much at the local store, and you can see it on the faces of the store owners. They'll survive another year, but it won't be easy. A young kid comes in with fifty cents for candy. In the summer, that would've been at least a fifteen-dollar purchase for a family. Sol switched cars with his buddy and was now driving a sweet BMW SUV. He couldn't get the seat positioned correctly, and the driver behind him was getting impatient at the stop sign. Sol was chuckling, though, because this seat situation was getting ridiculous. He was lying back too much and hunched over and uncomfortable with his feet above his knees!

What kind of car was this? Sol wondered as the driver behind him decided to lay on the horn for a second time. Finally, Sol just had to go now and hit the gas and figure out the seat on the way. The highway markers for the exits and nearby cities were floating holographic images. This was really confusing to him and at the same time so cool. Some people like driving this way. He did not. His car flipped upside down, and this was making it even harder to navigate the signage. He figured out the seat position, found his lane and settled in for a long drive.

Sol arrived at the house. It was vast inside with spacious rooms, yet somehow down to earth and very comfy feeling. His old work colleague was playing "Songbird" by Fleetwood Mac on the piano. It sounded beautiful and the notes echoed throughout the house. The conference was almost over, and Sol just had one last speech about resilience that he had to deliver to the outgoing group. They were losing attention, as they had been there for days. He had the entire audience empty their minds and sit in group silence for a few moments before he began his last talk. This emptiness and renewed sense of being present seemed to give the audience as well as himself a much-needed boost of energy and awareness.

THE WORK

Beginner's Mind

I went for a five-mile run this morning and at about the halfway mark, I started feeling tired. My legs felt heavy, and my form was off. I shifted my focus from thoughts of being tired and my body to the feeling of my foot hitting the ground directly under me, a principle of ChiRunning that I learned while becoming certified as an instructor. Then I shifted to focusing on trees in my line of sight. I approached the various trees with the not-knowing attitude. It's hard at first. I looked at and studied trees as I ran by them and wondered how old each tree was and what kind of tree it was.

First, it made my thoughts of feeling tired go away, which was my goal. Second, it helped me on my study of what is true and real. My thoughts about feeling tired were not true and real. The trees were true and real. Something super interesting happened during this experience. I kept going back to the trees, observing without knowing, and my mind kept wanting to label the tree. It was as if my mind was interrupting and getting in the way of the truth and reality of the tree.

So, then I pretended I was existing long ago, before the invention of words. How would I approach this tree based upon not knowing, a true image from *Zen Mind Beginner's Mind* for those of you that have read that fabulous book by Shunryū Suzuki. The book is one of my all-time favorites to read or listen to on audio as his voice pure

Zen as well. As I approached each tree with a beginner's mind, the trees started becoming super interesting and unique. The bark was interesting, the way the leaves were growing, how many branches, etc. Again, it's super hard not to label things. Before words, how would I know if the tree was tall or short, dead or alive, big or small, or two branches or three branches? I realized how much our thinking and labeling and words get in the way of life sometimes. Of truly experiencing reality and being free in the moment.

So many more possibilities opened for me during these experiences when I stopped labeling. I think we label to try to make sense of things, to understand things better, for more control, but it doesn't work. It actually does the opposite. Then I applied this same approach to my thoughts of being tired. However, I did this in conjunction with how my body was feeling. In other words, this is not an intentional distraction that you are aiming toward. It is actually a check-in with reality, where I could validate whether or not my thoughts were accurate against the truth of what my body was really telling me. Wow, what an epiphany, as my thoughts were so unreal and not the truth! As Wim Hof says, "Let the body do what the body is capable of doing." This means, don't let your mind shortchange your body's ability to persevere. My body was telling me that I had more in my tank and that my thoughts were simply a distraction to get me to stop. Not only that, a huge benefit was that I forgot about time and running itself. Next thing I knew, my run was almost over!

July 2013

Sol had been sitting at the airport bar for a few hours now. He had to; there was nothing else to do and nowhere else he could go. The snow had delayed so many flights, and many were even canceled until tomorrow. All of a sudden, a few of his friends from years ago came up behind him and joined him at the end. They talked for a while. After an hour or so, Sol abruptly left. Just stood up and walked away without saying goodbye. He even forgot his wallet and phone at the bar. His friends were confused, and they didn't understand what had happened. Sol just needed to get out of there.

He saw the group from afar and heard that they may be filming in town. Their show has been the most popular streaming series in the past few years, especially with the teen crowd. Which is odd, because the show outdates them. He walked over toward the hot tub and thought, *What the heck. I'll just join them.* At first, there were only a few from the group in the tub, and he didn't recognize them. But others joined and he got a glimpse into how well this group of actors gelled with each other, on and off the stage. Just then, a man walked in front of them about a hundred feet away. He didn't look good. He stopped and bent over and then proceeded to throw up all over the ground. His head made a horrid jerking motion, swinging way back and then forward, multiple times. The actor on his right didn't skip a beat and continued on with his story about the fraternity brothers charged with changing lightbulbs as part of a hazing ritual. Sol realized that life was going to throw him curveballs every now and then, and that the most important thing was how he would choose to react to those unexpected and often unwanted situations.

Don't Quit

In 2023, I went through an experience that I don't wish on anyone. It was about freedom and losing my freedom. It was about violating my basic rights as a human being. It was about lack of accountability by those in power. It was about physical abuse and lack of ethics and morals. On the day of my trial, my attorney said in my ear, "You're in the system now. You don't want to be in the system. Get the fuck out of the system as soon you can. They play in the system every day, all day. They know the game. You don't." So, I got the fuck out of the system as soon as possible. My attorney was right; you don't want to be in the system … ever.

This morning, an immense wave of amazement came over me for getting through 2023 and for also managing to still live my life to my best extent possible. I didn't quit on myself or my children even though I had many reasons and opportunities to do so. I am so proud of myself for surviving this. So proud. While I wouldn't wish that experience on anyone, I have grown from it and learned so much about myself and others.

This poem helped me a lot, and I wanted to share it with you. To this day, I still don't know how I stumbled across it.

Don't Quit
Edgar A. Guest

When things go wrong, as they sometimes will,
When the road you're trudging seems all uphill,
When the funds are low and the debts are high,
And you want to smile, but you have to sigh,
When care is pressing you down a bit,
Rest if you must, but do not quit.
Life is queer with its twists and turns,
As every one of us sometimes learns,
And many a failure turns about,
When he might have won had he stuck it out;
Don't give up, though the pace seems slow –
You may succeed with another blow.
Often the goal is nearer than
It seems to the faint and faltering man,
Often the struggler has given up,
When he might have captured the victor's cup,
And he learned too late when the night slipped down,
How close he was to the golden crown.
Success is failure turned inside out-
The silver tint of the clouds of doubt,
And you never can tell how close you are,
So, stick to the fight when you're hardest hit –
It's when things seem worst that you must not quit.

April 2001

Sol remembered her from high school as being absolutely beautiful and incredibly quiet. He wondered what she was doing in this department store, at this time of year and this time of day. For him, this was normal behavior to be there. Sol watched her for a second, but then parted ways as she headed out to another store. He ended up at the men's department sale section, as usual, flipping through suits. He found one that fit him, a thirty-two short, even though he wasn't really in the market for a new suit. The man next to him was commenting about the suits, and Sol told the man that these were priced nicely. He also told him that a handmade version of this exact suit would cost at least ten times as much as this one. The store clerk nodded in complete agreement, hoping for the sale.

Years ago, Sol wore the handmade version of these suits and looked the part, but he was miserable. Very miserable. He left the suit rack and hit the cafeteria before meeting his friend for a bite to eat. The Pepsi machine was broken. Sol loves Pepsi; there's something about the sugar taste that gave him the craving. It's a different kind of taste than Coke, less sugary in his opinion. He grabbed a different drink and a bag of mixed nuts and was heading to the register to pay. He hadn't seen his friend in years, and he was looking forward to catching up.

Sol and his friend head out for the evening. It had been snowing for almost a day straight now. At least a foot had gathered outside on the ground, turning the neighborhood into a quiet, peaceful winter wonderland. Wendy had lost her earning, and it was pure gold. He just got home from work, and while walking up the steps to the porch, he saw it shimmering and about to fall through the cracks in the wooden floor. He handed it to her, and a smile came across her face that lit up the snowy street. He went inside to get ready for his lacrosse meeting; he was coaching another year of his son's club lacrosse team.

Sol continued to undress, undoing his tie and hanging it up along with his pant suits and jacket. He always enjoyed this part of the process, as he felt he was transforming and coming back to himself. He hit the bathroom and noticed a new toilet seat, yet the floor was wet from overflow. The room was full of parents of the kids he was about to coach for the season, and he was ready to talk schedules and upcoming practices, one of which started today in the snow. Someone behind him made a racist comment, and it took him by surprise. Typically, this group of parents is a good group of people, but new families often join this club team.

THE WORK

Affirmations

I want to share some of the work I have done over the past thirty years. Below are my unedited affirmations that I had subliminally recorded onto a meditation track using a program called Holosync over twenty years ago when my best friend Kerr, who wrote the forward to this book, and I were knee-deep into the program. Holosync, created by Bill Harris at the Centerpointe Research Institute, was somewhat new at the time, and it was an exciting time of exploration and personal growth for both me and Kerr.

These affirmations were written by me. They mean a lot to me. At the time, I believed to some extent that much of it was wishful thinking and that it wouldn't happen to me. I wasn't worth it. Not me. I am absolutely amazed to this day that most of this has come true for me. Absolutely floored. Please keep doing the work. Don't ever stop. You're worth it and you will be so happy you did. The universe is listening to the energy that you put out there through your thoughts and emotions. Our individual consciousnesses are connected to the greater conscious of the universe. We are made of energy, and it is scientifically proven that our hearts produce more energy than our brains.

My Holosync Affirmations

I am filled with love and gratitude. I believe in myself. I have the abilities, resources, talents, and skills to create my desired results. I am lovable and capable. I am worthy of love, joy, and success. I am attracting all the right people into my life. I make wise choices. I can create anything I want. I can handle anything that life hands me. I have all the energy I need to do everything I want to do. I make a lot of money, and I am a good father and husband. I can do both and enjoy my life.

I always come up with unlimited creative ideas to prosper. I am realizing my full potential each and every day. I am energetic and enthusiastic. I exude massive amounts of energy and enthusiasm. I am world-renowned author. My words and actions heal, and I am a restorer of faith and spirit.

I am beautiful, capable, and lovable. I am valuable. All my needs are met. I love myself unconditionally and nurture myself in every way. I give and receive love. I am an important and valuable part of the world. I am perfect just the way I am. My needs are important. It is easy and safe for me to know and express my feelings. It is safe to be vulnerable because the universe protects me.

I like people, and I radiate warmth and friendship to all. The world is a safe and nurturing place. People like me. I can set healthy boundaries for myself. I am healing all my childhood wounds and moving toward greater peace and happiness every day.

My fears are melting away, and my happiness is growing to infinite proportions. I speak my truth and walk my talk. My capacity to give and receive love grows by the minute. I release my past and welcome the present. My happiness comes from within.

No one has the power to make me feel bad. I am a good person. I can trust. I can hope. I can be curious and explore and do. I am somebody. I have purpose and value. I can imagine and feel. I have conscience. I am intelligent. I can think and learn.

June 2008

The waitress walked over toward Sol's table, where he had just sat down. The table was empty except for a few napkins. In fact, the restaurant was fairly empty as well. When she got to the table, she proceeded to wipe the table down and ask him what he wanted to drink. She offered him a beer list, and he opted for his usual, a Guinness. She then proceeded to leave him a stack of cash on the table. He said "Sorry, I just got here, this isn't my money." He hadn't taken a sip of the beer yet, but he knew inside it violated his sobriety.

It was unclear how many times he had done this and whether he was truly sober. He knew he had to meet his friends later that night, after everyone had completed their yard work. When he got home, he saw his buddy through the side window of the house. He was digging a hole for his addition to his driveway. Sol was looking forward to spending time with his friends tonight. It had been a while.

While standing in line at the restaurant waiting to pay with his friend, Sol decided that he would bring back the food for his kids, who hadn't eaten dinner yet. Sol stepped up to order when it was his turn and ordered the special of the day. He had never been to this part of the restaurant before, so after his order, he simply moved to the left and waited ... and waited. Finally, his friend told him that he needed to go down the register and pay while the food was being prepared. Then he would come back to the counter and pick up his meal.

Sol walked down toward the cash register. Once there, the man working the cash register asked him his full name, first and last. Odd, he thought, for simply buying a lunch. But the clerk typed the name into his system anyway. Then the clerk proceeded to thread a sewing needle with the aims of handing it over to him. Sol couldn't recall if the sewing needle was his or the clerk's. He thought it was his own. The clerk threaded the needle perfectly on his first try.

He'd done this many times before. After the clerk was finished, he handed him the needle with the string attached so that he could carry it easily. He wondered more about the sewing needle. Sol wondered what the needle could symbolize in his life right now.

THE WORK

Forgiveness

One of the most impactful tools that I have used to help me forgive others who have hurt me in some way is the meta kindness loving prayer. My version goes like this, and I say it for four different people. The first person is myself, then someone I love deeply, then a complete stranger, and finally someone who hurt me. The last person can be very difficult at times to pray for, and it makes it a bit easier if you remember that we are all connected at a very deep energy level.

> May I (you) be happy
> May I (you) be healthy
> May I (you) be safe
> May I (you) be free from suffering

Forgiveness helps reduce your number of dark moments. I learned this the hard way. It took me awhile to truly forgive those involved who hurt me during my divorce and during my incident in 2023. But when I finally did, wow, did a lightness enter my life. I felt a hundred pounds lighter walking around. I created an inner space of freedom and choice in myself after I forgave. Now, I had so many more options because my behavior wasn't being driven by an unseen anger or sadness or resentment anymore. Holding on to resentment and anger truly is like the second arrow in Buddhist texts. The first arrow comes from the people who hurt you, and the second arrow is from yourself and causes unnecessarily suffering. Do yourself a huge favor, remove any second arrows in you as soon as you can through the work and the way. It is one of my biggest hopes that this book helps you, or anyone, do this. That's how impactful it was to me when I did this.

One of my proudest moments though was when my kids experienced and understood what I did through forgiveness. Wow, what an amazing skill I just modeled for them and a wonderful example I set that will hopefully stick with them throughout their lives. The ability to forgive. And move on. It is so human, yet so hard to do. It did take me a few years, actually. And there were times where I said, "Yeah, I definitely forgive both of them," and then shortly after my behavior or words told a different story.

So, I kept working at it over time. I read books on forgiveness. I meditated on my experiences up until that time. I battled between forgiving as an act for just myself or for them. Turns out, it was for both me and for them. And I know it was for them because of the response I received from them both, one verbally, the other tacit. Living life with an open heart and from a place of love has never led me astray.

Again, more irony. I love it! And listen, you've heard the saying that forgiveness doesn't mean forgetting. Well, that's true, and I guess that's our lot as humans. If our goal is staying present in each moment as much as possible without living in the past, then forgiveness is a necessity. When I remember what happened, I live in the past. I don't want to live in the past. I want to enjoy my current experience in the "now" as much as possible. Forgiveness has helped me do this really well. I pray the same can happen for you on your path.

November 1999

Sol couldn't believe it was time to vote again, as this was his third trip out voting in the past several months. The rules were changing lately for elections. He arrived at the building that he thought was his voting area. He went inside, searching around for signs and a kind, older woman noticed that he was lost and pointed him in the right direction. Sol descended the round stairs to the bottom floor of the building. *Ah, yes, this all looked vaguely familiar,* he thought, as he dipped his fingers in a bowl of crab dip, licked his fingers, and proceeded to go inside to vote.

The voting took much longer than he had anticipated, causing him to be late for yet another run. This one was a 10K race back in his hometown. While driving to the race location, Sol realized that he was wearing jeans. Meaning he would have to run in jeans. He thought, *What the hell?* He had his AirPods, which he thought would be good enough. As he arrived at the race start, the runners had left just seconds ago. John, who was in charge of the event, told him he could make it if he wanted. But Sol knew he needed a chip for his shoe, and he just wasn't going to be ready in time.

He decided to opt out of the race. He watched the runners round the first turn, racing out of sight. He was at peace with his decision. He decided to meet everyone afterward at the after party. The house looked vaguely familiar, yet he had never been in it before. He looked around after sitting at the table to chat, admiring the furniture and the architecture of the place. It was a beautiful home indeed. The rooms were expansive. The flow of the home was perfect. He complimented the owners on their beautiful home.

THE WAY

Wim Hof Method

> So ... why don't you go with me, into the depths of
> the brain. It's all showing, it's all there man.
> —Wim Hof

I learned the Wim Hof method about five years ago because I'm somewhat of a nut and like to push the boundaries of what my mind and body can experience and endure with the goal of making the most out of my life. I started with the Wim Hof Method app on my phone and followed all his daily challenges, because it was fun earning the badges over time and it kept me engaged when the going got tough, which it certainly did. I also completed his introductory class online which was self-study and included watching videos of Wim teaching a small group of people.

Here are some of the health benefits that I have picked up over the years. Keep in mind I still do cold showers and his retention breathing every single day, and I also have a portable ice pod out back! If you want to feel like you drank ten coffees but without the anxiety and actually feel energized and in an amazing mood ... then do some ice baths. I'm not going to lie, the first thirty seconds or so are challenging, but if you do the breathing properly you will soon sink into an amazing place of stillness with your mind. It is truly transformational.

The benefits include improved skin complexion, lower blood pressure, decreased inflammation, better blood circulation, quicker recovery times from running and yoga, increased breathing capacity on runs, better overall mood, more daily energy ... just to name a few.

There's a point on the Wim Hof app during retention breathing when Wim says, "And just be in this moment." I've used this saying many times in waking life to settle my emotions and reground myself internally so that I am not swayed by external events. It has settled me down so many times and has enabled me to stay present with myself and less reactive. Thank you, Wim Hof!

March 1997

Sol wasn't sure why this man was spilling his guts in front of this specific group of people. This wasn't the time nor the place, but the man continued on. Maybe he was trying to lighten the mood of the group. After all, they were searching for clues for a missing person in the community. Yet here he was, this total stranger, explaining to the entire group how his ex-wife cheated on him and with whom. He spared no details, none. The group was completely engaged while this man continued his story. Yet, surprisingly to everyone there, the man was completely unemotional about the whole series of events. In fact, it appeared that he had a small grin as he completed his story.

It was Sol's turn now, and he was nervous, very nervous. Everyone had already gone before him, and they all seemed to nail their routines. As he walked through his doorway and toward the curtain, he started to get very anxious, and he couldn't remember his jokes! *How did everyone else do it*, he thought to himself. *Did they write the jokes down? Have a teleprompter?* But it was too late for this, as he was about to walk through the curtain into the arena.

It was a round domed arena with seats all along the outside.

He couldn't believe he was going to do this, but he decided to ad lib. Sol told the joke about the bear and the rabbit taking a shit in the woods. You know, the one about the shit not sticking to the rabbit's fur? Ah, well that's for another day then. As Sol was continuing, he wasn't sure exactly how it the joke ended. He was the only one who did not stick to the script. The judging came in. He won! He knocked the judges over. They called it a masterpiece of authenticity and delivery. Sol couldn't believe what he just heard.

THE WORK

Choice and Curiosity

I can choose each morning to continue to create my own needless suffering, or I can change my life's momentum by spending the first thirty minutes of my morning in meditation and intention setting. I can choose to complain over the wrapper left on the floor by my child the night before, or I can mindfully pick it up with love and throw it away. What a difference that makes in the next ten minutes of my day. And, most likely, a ripple effect for the rest of my day both internally and how I interact with others. And, most likely, a ripple effect for the rest of my life. That is part of what karma is all about to me. Daily actions, thoughts, and intentions that play out in the future. Could be good, could be bad. We get what we put out to the universe, even if we aren't aware of what we're putting out there. Contemplate that one for a few minutes. It's scary and exciting at the same time. So much yin and yang in our existence.

In our internet era, there is so much information out there to help us live our lives and become better, more loving people. So many religions and spiritual practices that you can turn to. I have discovered an underlying connection between them all, and that connection is love. So why not focus on love first and foremost? Why not love yourself first, so that you can learn to love others? Take care of yourself first, so that if the situation demands it, you can take care of someone else.

Go for a walk on an early Sunday morning in midspring. No one is out. There's no wind in the air, and the trees are completely still. The birds are active. Notice the unique energy surrounding each tree. They all have some type of energy field. Get in close. Notice that some of the buds haven't blossomed yet. How do they know what to do? How do trees grow the way they do? What is behind the scenes there? And we say trees are living or dead. What does living mean? Do we simply mean growing; the tree grows, so that means it's alive? We certainly don't mean that the tree has consciousness. Or do we? Is a tree aware that it is growing and alive? How would we ever know that? Does it matter? Can we measure that somehow? Can we measure consciousness—both the existence of it and the density of it?

March 1985

Sol came up to the street in the middle of the town, but the street was closed off for the running race that day. The timer board was set up as well as tape to keep the spectators off the street, so he was forced to make his way through a mob of people, and then the rest of the way was indoors. The path took Sol in and out of various houses and stores, and when he entered the last store, he noticed an older man sitting in his pool inside of his condo area. The condo was vast, open, and beautiful. Not much furniture, but what was there was exquisite.

The old man made a weird gurgling sound and then blew his snot to the left into the pool. Sol was pretty grossed out by this and continued through the condo to get back to the outside in a hurry when he noticed a stand that had amazing large pearls on them. Sol was blown away by the beauty and size and vividness of each singular pearl on display. He had never known that they could be so beautiful. As he continued on his path, Sol noticed an older lady in the same condo area selling expensive laundry detergent in her name. *So amazing,* Sol thought to himself as he passed the display, finally arriving outside after about an hour or so or making his way through the buildings. Once there, Sol spotted his friend who was flying his robot drone that they made together over the past few months. They also just found out that a company had offered to buy the design and patent for an incredible price in the hopes that they can make a larger-than-life size robot drone that others will be able to use and benefit from. This made Sol really happy.

You Have Always Been the Answer

You are wonderful. You always have been. You are not lost. You are the answer.

If you feel that this is nonsense talk, or that you are an exception to the statements above, then it's time to roll up your sleeves and do the work. It's not physically demanding work. You're not going to sweat and lose weight doing this work. At the same time, it may be the hardest and longest and most impactful project you will ever work on in your lifetime.

You have an amazing window of opportunity to discover the truth about yourself. To live freely and lightly and lovingly. But beware, that amazing window of opportunity is not as long as you think it is. We have been blessed with a body, a soul, a heart, and a brain for as long as we are on this beautiful planet. There is so much to be grateful for while we are here. So very much. I believe it is an absolute miracle that we are here on this planet along with every other species and plant.

However, it is very difficult to get to this understanding without doing the work. In fact, throughout the work I have done on myself in this amazing lifetime, it is more than an understanding. It is an experience of life itself. A pure experience. An experience of clarity. An experience of excitement and passion and hope. An experience of pure love and bliss inside of me. Do I have days where I lose sight of this? You bet I do. But the work has enabled me to recenter myself internally much faster than I was able to do in my younger years, even five to ten years ago.

July 2024

So many questions pop up for Sol during his walk by himself, questions he doesn't have answers to. That frustrates him. So, he sits for a bit. He sits with himself, in silence. He creates a space for the answers, for the way, to appear. Sol quiets everything, and gives the way a space to show itself, in some form or another. He is patient; he has to be. He has no other choice, or at least he doesn't want that choice. He knows enough to realize that is true.

Maybe Sol is the problem. Maybe he's in the way. Maybe he is blocking the answer, not on purpose, but simply because he thinks he is the one who has the answer. He thinks he has to find the answer through force, by doing a certain something or thinking a certain way.

So, he realized that there is nothing to do but be.

Give It Back to the Universe
When You're Done with It

If you are a seeker like me, have you ever asked yourself what are you really searching for? Have you sat down and thought about that question? Are you searching for happiness and comfort and a feeling of being OK, safe, and loved? Are you not sure what specifically you are seeking but feel that once you find "it" everything will be good, and you can stop searching? If you do the work, you will experience glimpses of it, if you're aware and open enough to listening. But the human condition is an impermanent one with ups and downs, forward and backward, and positive and negative. You take the good with the bad, the bad with the good. Then you give it all back to the universe, freeing yourself up for the next experience and then the next one.

I sit outside and small bird flits near me and lands on the sidewalk in front of me, hopping quickly and pecking at the grass next to the walkway. And another bird joins in the fun. Two birds simply being, existing in peace together. They are not bothered by me right now, as I write this on my front porch. The more I watch the birds, it seems more and more stillness and quietness enters my mind and body. I'm not thinking about my work meetings later today or what I may have to do this weekend. Then in a flash, the birds are gone. So, I give the birds back to the universe and feel grateful for those few moments of clarity and peace during their short visit.

August 2008

Sol walked down the hallway of the school to the second classroom, where the teacher was taking roll in the first classroom. He barely could make out his name when it was called, and then he yelled, "Here" down the hallway. Next up were the questions that the teacher would ask him. She wanted Sol to name three other athletes who had recently passed away who also had memorials made for him or her. One of the names was Michael Jordan, and the memorial was a large 737 airliner. Weird, he thought. Jordan is still living. Even with the help of his friend, he could not figure out a single answer. The teacher gave him the first one: Robert Parrish from the Boston Celtics. They seemed to be all basketball players, he surmised. He failed the pop quiz, nonetheless. *What kind of class is this?* he wondered as the teacher moved on to the next student.

Still thinking of what he might do tonight, he left class and headed down the hallway to the group discussion. The auditorium was crowded and dark. Not a seat was empty. The line he was in was moving quickly through the rows of seats. Everyone was there to shake Frank Sinatra's hand. As the line moved through the aisles, he recognized many of his old coworkers. He threw a paper wad at one of his pals down a few rows, and his current boss gently elbowed him in line, hinting at this wasn't the place for that. As they approached Sinatra, the line sped up even faster. So fast, that when he got to Sinatra, he was only able to quickly shake his hand. He didn't even get to see his face because of the darkness and speed of the line. In fact, the line was moving so fast that they all crashed into the wall right next to Sinatra's aisle seat!

The Biggest Freedom

We put so much pressure on ourselves daily. We often take way too much responsibility for things that aren't ours to hold. Boundaries, boundaries, boundaries! One of the most important things I learned while attending Adult Children of Alcoholics is that I am not responsible for other people's behaviors or reactions. This is what I mean by boundaries. I am responsible for my own behavior and my reactions to my life experiences. I am not responsible for anyone else's happiness or sadness or anger. This doesn't mean that I don't care about people and what they are going through, I most definitely do. It means I do not inappropriately take on the heaviness of what they are going through. That is their side of the street, and they are responsible for that. My side of the street is my responsibility.

We don't need to watch and scrutinize every minute detail of our behavior. This inner critic can be excruciating at times. Our false selves have been both the super-achieving perfectionist as well as the addict in the alley. We often have difficulty identifying and expressing our individual thoughts, wishes, and feelings. Don't feel alone or weird if you experience any of the above (or *all* in my case!). It's part of our human condition. Keep doing the inner work on yourself. Don't give up. The more you do the work on a day-to-day basis, the freer you will feel yourself becoming over time.

Problems that seemed incredibly important in the past won't seem that important anymore. Dwelling on bad feelings and ruminating will ease off as well.

This, to me, is one of the biggest freedoms—the freedom to understand how much all of our thoughts, feelings, and emotions are like birds singing. They come and go, come and go, come and go, and we needn't do anything about it if we don't want to. In fact, there's nothing to do about the singing of the birds except to enjoy it for the short time that you are blessed by it. Just like the birds singing, we don't control when and where some of our thoughts come from. So just realize that thoughts will come out of nowhere, stay for a time, and then fly away just like a bird. There is nothing at all we need to do about that except understand it. That to me is freedom.

February 1993

The purpose seemed clear, but didn't make any sense at the same time. Sol knew what they had to do; he just had no idea why they were doing it. A long, white plastic tube was protruding from the ground. Sol peered inside and down the length of the wide tube, where he saw pieces of slate rock making up the inside of the hole down below. He took a shovel and banged out some of the pieces sticking out, the ones that would block their progress. And then they began, one by one, pulling up pieces of long, thin sheet metal from the dank basement floor and then dropping them down the hole.

Apparently, they finished in record time, beating the previous team by over five minutes. The timer couldn't believe it and went to talk to the judge about the results. Sol grabbed a bottle of beer and hopped down onto the dusty basement floor to walk around and check out what was left, and then headed out toward the boardwalk.

He walked along the sand. It was a beautiful day at the beach. One of those days where the sun is out strong, and the clouds are huge and white. He passed a younger girl struggling to pull something in on her line. She was struggling for a few minutes, and as he looked back toward her, he saw the head of a good-sized shark pop up. "You caught a shark. Keep working it and be careful!" he shouted in her direction.

Sol came to the end of the beach and noticed large crowd of people had gathered. As he neared, he could hear the conversations more clearly. A young boy had fallen off the edge of the cliff, down a hundred feet to his death. People were beside themselves and grieving as it had just happened. It was a terrible accident. The worst of any kind at the beach in many years.

When he got to his car, Sol called up his brother, who was trying to stop dipping tobacco. He told his brother that his son won't stop dipping until he does. Then his brother took him by surprise by saying, "I'm done. I'm quitting drinking too. I've giving it all up for a while." He had never been prouder of his brother in his life. Well, other than the time his brother stood up to the neighborhood bully when they were in middle school.

THE WAY

Imperfection and Dating

Let's talk a little bit about perfection. Or better yet, let's talk about imperfection. Settle into the fact that as human beings, we are imperfect. That includes me and that includes you. It took me many years to not only understand this, but also to believe it deep down inside of me so that I could stop dragging myself through the mud unnecessarily when things weren't perfect. Imperfection also includes your favorite actor or actress, favorite athlete, and favorite role model. So, right away, drop the idea of the being the "perfect single dad" or the "perfect worker" or the "perfect stay-at-home mom." Just accept this right away, right out of the gates. Accept it every day if you have to. Write it down so you see it every day. You will be doing yourself a big favor, and you will also notice that your anxiety around striving to be perfect will gradually fade to the background. This is huge, if you really think about. Give yourself this gift.

A therapist once told me in the very beginning of my divorce to find relationships where I don't need anything from someone. At first, I was like what does that even mean? Then I was like, OK thanks, I'll keep that in mind. But I didn't really hear what he was saying. I hear it now though, loud and clear. After twenty-three years in that relationship, I dove back into dating. Probably too soon. But there was no way my buddy Jimbo was not going to set up a dating profile for me online. Getting back into dating allowed me to put myself out there and try to love again. It was hard. I got hurt badly in the divorce. I was clunky at first, and I feel that after eight years I am starting to understand what giving and receiving loving means.

I've meditated on it a lot and read tons of books. Yes, I mean reading books about what loving someone means. It's just that I thought I must not have gotten it right because of the divorce. What I really learned was that I needed to love myself first and to open up again and trust again. I don't think I got the loving part right, though. I don't necessarily regret dating so quickly after my divorce, but I do recommend spending time thinking about it if you're ever in that situation. Take some time to figure out what love means to you and what is important in a relationship. I identified my top five needs in a relationship, and it was really helpful. Kindness and compassion are at the top of my list. Every situation is different, every human has a different story. You just have to know yourself and what you are actually seeking in the relationship and also what you have to give.

What's the point of regret, anyway? It's not like if I went back in time, I would have done something differently. I'd do the exact same thing again with the knowledge I had during that time, because again we're only human beings. Looking back, I thought I was taking care of myself by dating and felt that if I was in relationship and loving someone else, I would feel good about myself. Simply said, I was looking for validation outside of myself. Although I felt like I did at the time, I now realize that I didn't need another person to help me feel good inside. I thought I did, but I now know the truth that everything is an inside job. And the better you are at the inside job, the more beautifully you will shine on the outside. The other thing I wasn't good at was being loving in my relationships. It wasn't for a lack of effort or a lack of caring. I really did try, and I really did care.

What my therapist was saying to me was this: "Go mend your wounds from the divorce. Don't take your wounds into a relationship with another woman right now." I didn't listen. I loved the best I could, but maybe I just wasn't ready yet for it yet and needed to do more inner work first. I've been in a serious relationship now for seven months. I am truly able to address my issues and wounds. I will continue to work on myself as the universe thinks that I am ready for another relationship. Some days it's hard to be alone and go to sleep at night by myself. Other days it feels exactly right. Either way, I am not perfect. I will continue to make mistakes and don't always expect roses and rainbows anymore. However, I am truly learning what it means to love someone and accept someone's love.

August 1989

The elevators ran up to the 250th floor, and Sol never knew that a building could be this tall. There was an elevator just for children, but apparently anyone could use it. Go figure. He arrived at the elevator just as a wedding party got on and filled up the elevator on the left. The right one had just left. Sol pressed the up button too early, and the door opened back up on the wedding party. *Oops, sorry*, he thought, a bit embarrassed. He finally got on the left one when it came back down a few minutes later. When he got to the hallway, he saw the mess that he had to help clean up.

They packed everything into boxes and cartons, and then into a shopping cart. It all barely fit, including the video arcade stand-up game. You know. The really big ones that you would find in an arcade. And, shockingly, it all fit in the elevator for the ride back down to the lobby. His friend decided to do the video game description to those in the elevator. He held her by the legs as she stood on the arcade game, her voice cracking because she was afraid to fall. She went on though. The online messages started flowing into the screen of the arcade game. Users were asking great questions. One user asked, "How does the game know you ordered a pizza the first time you played?" Great question!

After arriving downstairs, they loaded the equipment into her car, and she peeled away. Sol walked toward the sunset. It was beautiful. He had a question for God that he had wanted to ask for a long, long time. The sun was God to him in that moment. He climbed to a higher point on the hill to get a better view of the sun, which was setting fast, so he hurried a bit more. Sol felt much better after his conversation with God. He then found his car and proceeded to drive toward the freeway ramp.

THE WORK

Do We Need a Reason?

Why do we have to wait for something to make us smile? Why don't we just smile for no reason other than to smile? You feel good when you smile, don't you? Why don't we do it more then? Let's smile more. Let's love more. Let's give more.

Why do we worry about things that haven't happened yet? What's that all about? Why, on a Sunday evening when the rain is falling peacefully outside, do we start to worry about Monday's workday? Why not enjoy the rain? Why ruin the present moment by worrying about the meetings on Monday? Or thinking that you don't enjoy your job, and what's it all for?

Instead of worrying about work tomorrow, go stare at a flower outside and enjoy the beauty and life that it magically creates. Why on earth, pun intended, do we consider that a waste of time? Why is worrying about work more important than appreciating a flower? Am I going to fail in life if I enjoy the flower for a few moments, instead of worrying about work? I'd argue the opposite. I'd say you'll be more productive the next day. Why aren't we OK with boredom? Why don't we just sit here and do nothing? Why do we worry about work instead? Or why do we run to the TV to watch a show? Why do we feel like utter failures if we slow down and do nothing but enjoy ourselves and the moment?

I was talking with a very good friend today who is feeling

the fast-paced society that we live in currently. It's taking a toll on people. We need to rest more, slow down a bit, spend time contemplating things more, and enjoy the beauty that we are so fortunate to be able to experience on a daily basis. It is a true miracle that we are alive on this planet. A true miracle. Let's make an effort to appreciate that fact more. I feel that if we do that, we would all be more loving and caring to each other, and happiness would spread like wildflowers. This is something our planet desperately needs.

Enjoy the moments before it's too late. Be happy with yourself. Love yourself. Celebrate yourself every single day. Smile a lot. Hug people. Share your gifts to the world. People want your gifts. Identify your gifts now. You have them. Don't wait until tomorrow. Ask someone what they are. Find your gifts. Share them like crazy. Don't let others bring you down. Don't get sucked into the emotional drama of other people. If you can't find any gifts to share, celebrate someone else's gifts.

As I mentioned earlier, I can choose each morning to continue to create my own needless suffering, or I can change my life's momentum and flip that script every morning I arise. I can choose to complain about the current heat wave hitting us this summer, or I can mindfully sit in the sun for five minutes in amazement and appreciation for what it gives us for free every single day. I can choose to check my phone the second I wake up in the morning, or I can meditate for thirty minutes in silence and set positive intentions for my day. We one hundred percent have the power to make these choices. Build these habits daily, and it will transform your life in ways you cannot even imagine right now.

April 1994

They just finished inspecting the final pieces of the tour. The large tree out front was perfect and had grown so much over the past years. The inside looks exquisite, from the newly re-etched stone frames to the alcoves. There were four or five of them. The lines carved into the stones were perfect, and they placed a memorial item into each spot. Sol quickly mulled over moving the fireplace to a different corner, but then decided against it.

The place looked amazing. Perfect, really. Afterward, Sol decided he was done here and headed down to the beach with his dog Frankie. As he was walking down the sandy path to the ocean, a few teenagers walked by him, dragging their boogie boards behind them in the sand. One bumped into Frankie, on purpose Sol thought, and then gave him some lip after walking by. He told the kid, "You don't want any of this." He heard the kids run into their parents, and cringed for a second, hoping one of the dads wouldn't come after him to start an argument. He continued down toward the beach. It was crowded today, much more crowded than most days at this time of year.

The large, long chest was left in the open field, right next to the tree line, and Sol was rummaging through it to carefully inspect all of the contents. He hadn't seen some of these things in years. A pair of old sunglasses, his favorite pants, and other keepsakes. His buddy walked behind him to talk to some of the other men in the area. "I hope you're not planning on leaving this thing out here in the grass to ruin my field," said one of them in the background. His friend walked by him again. She was sitting across from him in the lawn chair and looked his friend up and down, checking him out.

Sol let out an accidental audible tsk sound as she did this. "What?" she quizzed him. He told her it was nothing, which was a lie, and asked why she thought everything was about her. She got very upset at Sol, and as she walked away, she said loud enough for him to hear, "One of these days you're going to need something from me or want to talk."

He said, "No way."

She replied, "See, that proves my point."

After she left, Sol started dragging the large, awkward chest across the field until he came across the spot where he was supposed to store this thing. He noticed an older man tending to his part of the field, where there were newly planted seeds in the grass. He dragged the chest around this part. It was more work, and he wasn't sure the man appreciated or even noticed this kind gesture, but it made Sol feel good inside anyway.

Your Body is a Temple

Find your right exercise routine. I run and do hot yoga. I used to lift weights, but the older I get the less I want to build muscle. The natural body weight of yoga keeps my muscles in tone, and I haven't lifted weights in a few years now. Running suits me well, and I do feel that we are naturally supposed to move our bodies on a regular basis. I completed a six-month training program to become a certified ChiRunning instructor. It was exciting and scary at the same time! I have been running a lot of trails lately, as trails can be much softer on your feet during the landing phase of your running stride, as compared to pavement. In the fall, it gets cold and windy in Pittsburgh fairly quickly. The trails provide me shelter from the winds and make my runs much more enjoyable. Some mornings are so cold out that there are not a lot of other people on the trails during my morning runs. I could get a ten-mile trail run in and see one or two other people at most. I love it.

Trail running is one of my happy places. I have to stay alert and aware at all times. Too many roots, rocks, and leaves that can trip you up if you're not staying aware of what your body is doing. And that gels nicely with ChiRunning, because that is all about body sensing when you run so that you can run efficiently and injury free. There's also something amazing about running in nature, breathing in the rich oxygen that the trees produce and then seeing and hearing all the wonderful sounds and sights on the path.

Trail running is a lot like life. Sometimes on the tough uphills, I need to shorten my stride and slow down a bit. Sometimes on straightaways, I feel that the trail is running me. It's an out-of-body experience for sure, and I feel that I'm just floating effortlessly down the trail. And on downhills, I do both depending upon the terrain. Sometimes it's slow and controlled, and other times I am flying down there on autopilot and it's effortless. I turned fifty-two this past April.

I learned in tai chi how important your center is. Everything flows from your center, including your mind, balance, and power. As I mentioned earlier, your dantian is your energy center and where your chi resides. During my meditations, I often focus my breathing by placing my mind on my breath as it enters my nose, flows down to my dantian, and then up to my pineal gland. This circulation of breath and energy instantly gets me into a very positive energetic state and at the same time allows me to go very deep in stillness within myself.

The other activity I am religious about is yoga. I feel that I can't really put into words how important yoga is to me, as well as the Ignite Yoga community here in Pittsburgh. There are not a lot of men in these classes, which just boggles my mind. It is so good for our minds and bodies, including increased strength and flexibility, which has helped me tremendously in running. When I step onto my yoga mat in the studio, it's just me meeting myself on the mat. Plain and simple. There's nowhere to hide. No one is going to save you. Your teacher is not going to help you stay in eagle pose. It's all you. And it's why I love it so much. I've learned how much further I can push my mind and my body as well as how to body sense and feel my energy without thinking. I've become so much more flexible, both mentally and physically. There are times where I kind of disappeared while in class. I went somewhere. Not sure where. I know that may sound weird. But there have been brief moments of enlightenment. Of pure bliss and peace. I can't control when these moments come or for how long they stay. But, if I stay mentally and physically sharp, I can get better at not only recognizing these moments, but also at residing in the moment and existing without effort. Think about how hard life can be sometimes, and how much effort we put into living. Sometimes it's way too much effort. We have a hard time relaxing into life. We feel that if we're not powering through things then we won't accomplish shit, and we'll live a pointless life. I am experiencing the exact opposite. And yoga is helping facilitate it. I am experiencing that the less power and effort I put in, the more I can relax. The more I can relax—both mentally and physically—the more I can enjoy and thrive. When I stop forcing eagle pose, and I focus on the incredible internal power that I am, my thoughts go away, and I stand as one. Actually, I stand as one with everyone in the class. We are all one as we are all connected. On the other hand, I can also push my limits in yoga. Often, you will hear the teacher say, "or whatever is in your practice today," meaning know yourself and do the move how you see fit. In today's class, it was moving from a bridge to a wheel. I don't usually do wheels, but I wanted to push myself today, and it felt great. Other days in yoga, I don't push myself because it is not what my body needs on that particular day.

March 2019

Sol arrived at his friend's house the night before to stay for a few days and realized that he needed to wear a nice outfit, which he didn't bring. So, he went into his friend's room and picked out a pair of trousers that ended up fitting very well. As he turned around, Sol noticed a letter on the table, which he picked up even though his grandma always told him that nothing good comes from snooping.

Sol dropped the letter in complete shock after only quickly scanning a few lines. His best friend, it turns out, was working his ex-wife in an attempt to get more money out of the divorce settlement. His friend was furious and confronted her on this, and she simply said, "You're done. Toast." They argued, shouting and yelling at each other loudly. She picked up a laptop and swung it at his head, opening up a nasty gash that started quickly dripping blood. He grabbed his phone and made a few quick calls. Within an hour or so, he was on TV airing the latest incident. Her plan was over. Her social charm was quickly decreasing on the monitor with each word he spoke, until her support was gone. He won.

It was scary. He was scared. He knew the attacker was outside somewhere. Each window he passed and door he went by sent shivers up his spine. He never remembered being this afraid for his life before. Yet, he also knew he was inside a movie. But it was still super scary. He passed Madonna, said hello, and she smiled back. She was in a great mood tonight because she was hosting a dance party. The first group of dancers were called the Legs, and they had spider legs attached to their bodies. *They were not that good,* Sol thought to himself.

A Brief History of Me

I was born in Alamogordo, New Mexico, while my dad was stationed at Holloman Air Force Base in Albuquerque, New Mexico. We spent the next four years of my life living in New Mexico. The only things I remember from New Mexico are the White Sands, playing football, tarantula spiders, and my brother's and my fort out back where we used to dress up as cowboys, like my father and his brother, my Uncle Pudge, when they were little.

From there we moved to Dayton, Ohio. We attended a Catholic elementary school from first to fourth grade. I don't remember much about that time except Polish dancing and going to St. Alberts, where I went to a speech van for my R's and W's. I also got in trouble for chewing gum, and the priest made me wear the gum on my nose during classes. I also remember looking for snakes with one of my friends along the local highways. Also, our neighborhood was awesome. I had a friend next door, and we would play war with our army figures in sandboxes. We would also spy on his sister and really cool brother, who was into the band Kiss at the time. I also had a good friend across the street. We shared one super awkward but probably not so rare moment in the crawl space of the basement—I guess curious boys will be boys.

I had problems pronouncing my R's and W's. The speech therapist, I called her the lady, had me make the rooster sound putting my tongue on the top of my mouth to get down the R sound. It seemed to work well, although sometimes I still struggle with some R sounds.

From Dayton, we moved to Lionville, Pennsylvania, in 1980. We first lived in a townhouse, which none of us wanted to be in. My mom got something in her eye on Christmas Eve and had to go to the hospital. I did not like the kids at Lionville Elementary School. We played tetherball and had math contests, but I never really made good friends and didn't fit in at all. Ironically enough, I ended up playing travel soccer with Downingtown Spirit, and to this day it has been my favorite team of players to play sports with. Super-talented soccer players and outstanding dudes.

Thank God, my parents got a new house in Whitford Village, and we now would attend West Chester Area School District, specifically Mary C. Howse Elementary School. This is where I met the three best friends of my life—Matt Franks, Kerr Smith, and Jim Horan. We are still incredible friends to this day, and we would do anything for each other, even over forty years later! Granted, Matt didn't like me right away because I flipped my hat backward during our daily kickball game.

These friendships went on through Pierce Middle School, where Matt put a pencil through my wrist, and we all went to the sixth, seventh, eighth grade dances to hook up. We also attended many other parties. At the first one, we discovered weed. We also took bottle rockets up to the middle school dances in Lionville and shot them through the hallways of the dances! By the way, I had a separate set of friends with my brother in the neighborhood, and we discovered hard liquor (not beer), the choice for drink starting in the sixth grade. In fact, I had my first hangover from Jack Daniels and could not try that drink again until senior year in college at the Air Force Academy. My buddy Joe got me to bite the snake that bit me years ago and handed me the Jack Daniels during a trip to the University of Notre Dame, where we swear to this day that the dome is spray-painted gold (not real gold). We had many good years of lacrosse and friendships during these four years in college.

I am absolutely blessed to have these experiences with my friends. My friends kept me going through the terrible times growing up.

This book indeed is about me seeking a permanent solution to healing my childhood trauma, which I identified as the root cause of my addictions. If you suffer from trauma, many of the tools I share in this book will help you, I promise. It is, however, necessary to take the work very seriously, follow the way, and at the same time try to keep a lightness about you as go through your days. Not an easy thing to do at all, but I know in the deepest part of my heart that you can do this.

April 2022

Sol called her name a few times, each time a bit louder. But she didn't answer. Was she ignoring him? No, she would never; why would she? He knew it was her, though he hadn't seen his cousin Kim in many years. Yes, that was definitely her. He walked over the aisle of seats in the auditorium where she was sitting with her friends.

She apologized for not responding and they had a nice catch-up talk. Then, the ushers came and separated everyone into alternating seats due to COVID. After about ten minutes of conversation, he decided to walk around. He ran into the committee chair of the lacrosse fundraiser. It was his friend Eric, who he played club lacrosse with years ago. Eric was excited, but at the same time a bit overwhelmed. There must have been at least a thousand attendees at this event, and it was Eric's show. He let him go after a quick chat and wished him luck. The event lasted about two hours, and he began the process of starting his journey home on the metro.

Sol saw it happening in slow motion, and right away he knew it wasn't good. Finn, his four-month-old rottweiler puppy, hopped out of the eastbound metro car and ran quickly into the westbound car. The door closed quickly behind Finn, and the train was off. Sol was devastated and knew that was not good at all. Fortunately, he received help when his friends took turns in their own cars and others rode the trains. They checked all the stops. They walked the platforms and the buildings that connected to the roadways. Nothing.

Sol was beyond worried now and hopped into his friend's car, and they drove the town. For some odd reason, his friend spotted a house off the road a bit. They pulled into the gravel driveway, dust coming up from under the wheels of the car. They got out, and right away they noticed a family on the front porch. Next to the mom was an adult rottweiler. Maybe Finn ran here? This wasn't Finn's mom, but perhaps Finn thought it was. Sadly, Finn did not come here. Sol started to cry, and finally he just broke down and collapsed. He felt hope slipping out his fingertips, and there was nothing he could do.

THE WORK

Wash Yourself of Yourself (Rumi)

You know, I have been in a rut the past week and my workweek seemed impossible to get through. Not hard work. It was just hard to get through. I only wanted to get through the week, and when I get to that point, which doesn't happen very often, I know I'm in trouble. Then, someone pulled a super passive-aggressive stunt today, and it worked as it really got to me. I had some major shenpa, as Pema Chodron would say. I got hooked big time. The storyline grew and grew. I couldn't let it go. Waves of guilt passed over me and through me. I really started feeling sorry for myself, playing the victim. Again, never a good sign.

As they say, when the student is ready the teacher appears. Well, I decided to pick up my book on Rumi this evening and do some reading on the couch. Low and behold, this line came to me when I needed it badly: "Wash yourself of yourself." Wow. I read it to my daughter who is a freshman at college, and she was like, "Huh?" So, we had a good conversation about it.

When you start to feel really heavy, and life seems difficult and nothing seems to be in synch, just wash yourself of yourself. Forget about yourself for a while. After all, it is your "self" that is the problem anyway. So just forget about it for a bit. One thing that I learned that has helped me during these times is to visualize taking a washcloth and just washing yourself off yourself. Go ahead and do it. How does it feel? I immediately felt lighter, the tightness in my chest went away, and my head cleared a bit. I jumped on the piano for forty-five minutes and played some tunes and then played with my Rottweiler puppy, Finn. Got me back to the present moment and washed myself of myself. Thank you, Rumi.

June 1997

Sol was elated as he noticed many of his old teachers from high school were here. He hugged his lacrosse coach. He told his algebra teacher that he was his favorite of all time. He thanked his sister's coach for being there for her all the time. Then, the weirdest thing happened when Sol's friend got her hair caught in the wood on the ledge and she pulled it out and started crying. He knew it was time to get going, and he had so much fun seeing everyone.

There was one problem, though; he was drunk. His buddy just left and got home safely. *I can do it too,* he thought. But his buddy lives so close. Sol stumbled down the sidewalk and tripped and fell on his face. *Not good,* he thought. He got in his car and started driving, and it felt all wrong. He pulled into the nearest place he could find and parked his car. Time to walk home. He knew it would take forever, but he forged on. Then, he got lost. Out of nowhere he ran into another friend from the reunion. She helped him get closer to home. They were climbing scaffolding laddering when someone from below starting shooting harpoon-like arrows at them. They hit another person further away. Then, they aimed at his friend and hit her. She fell to her death. He climbed down to join the group, and decided he wanted to live with them forever. They were naturalists who lived off the land. He was sad, knowing that his parents would never see him again.

Sol held the three flowers in his hand. He was on his way to the mall. The petals on the flowers were blowing away in the wind, but he didn't care.

THE WAY

Coming Home

Some of the most powerful work and impactful visualizations I have experienced for me is when I walk up the street to the bus stop with my arm around my thirteen-year-old self. I have a picture of me from that exact time, standing on the driveway and holding a few textbooks under my arm. I know what I was going through in my life during that time. Someone took the picture; I don't remember who did, which is telling in and of itself. I do know I wasn't happy, as things were not good at home, and anger and sadness consumed me during those days. That was my trauma lot as a child. I didn't want the picture taken. I didn't want to be there. I didn't want to live in that house, in that environment, anymore.

In my visualization and meditations, I walk up the street where I grew up with my thirteen-year-old self with my arm around him. I talk with him. I tell him I know what he's going through. I ask him questions like, "Are you OK today?" "What's going on inside of you?" "What can I do to help you right now on this day?" "What does your school day look like today?" Then, I say things to him like, "You have such so much talent and a huge caring heart, and I see amazing things ahead for you in your life." I say, "I am always here for you" as I take my hand and mess rub the top of his head really quick and bring him in for a hug as we continue to walk. Sometimes we walk up the street and sometimes we pull letters

115

from thankful readers out of the mailbox. Other times, we go through a portal and visit my future self, and the three of us sit in union and talk and hug and heal.

I wrote this book because I made a promise to him. I promised him that all his pain would not go to waste. All his anger and suffering and sadness—the two of us would harness it and help others who are going through something similar, whether as a child or as an adult. I am so fucking proud of him for how he persevered through the war zone, how he managed to function through the brutal emotional abandonment and physical abuse. He was a tough, tough kid back then, and I am forever grateful for his perseverance and fortitude. I have learned so much from him.

I love you Jason, we did it, dude. Fuck yeah, we did it.

Acknowledgments

I express my deepest gratitude to the following amazing human beings for helping me stay open and vulnerable and for their support and guidance throughout my process of creating and sharing.

Thanks to my children, Riley, Sean, and Ian, the true loves of my life. You three have been through so much, and I am proud to call myself your dad.

Thanks to Maureen. As we continue to ride bikes together and protect our shared egg with conscious love, I love you.

Thanks to Carla, for going way past above and beyond with your editing skills, your time and energy, and your open-hearted, honest, and joyful approach to helping me. Forever *grateful*.

Printed in the United States
by Baker & Taylor Publisher Services